UNDERSTANDING PROBLEM GAMBLERS

Understanding Problem Gamblers

A Practitioner's Guide to Effective Intervention

PAUL BELLRINGER

FREE ASSOCIATION BOOKS / LONDON / NEW YORK

First published in 1999 by
Free Association Books
57 Warren Street, London W1P 5PA

A catalogue record for this book is available from
the British Library

ISBN 1 85343 462 0 hbk; 1 85343 463 9 pbk

Designed, typeset and produced for Free Association Books by
Chase Production Service, Chadlington OX7 3LN
Printed in the EU by J.W. Arrowsmith, Bristol

To Matthew and Nathan.
A source of great youthful encouragement.

Contents

Acknowledgements

There are many people who have through their contributions and comments made this book possible. I would like to record my thanks to them all. In particular I would like to mention Anne, for her constant support and encouragement; Gordon for his original inspiration; Tony for putting me right on some important issues; Mark for his sound help and advice; and Mick, Julia, Adrian, Fred, Phil and Kevin for the wisdom of their experience.

Foreword

Dr Mark Griffiths
Psychology Division, Nottingham Trent University

Back in April 1988 when I was a PhD student, Dr Stephen Lee and I organised the first conference on adolescent gambling in the UK at the University of Exeter. Of the fifty or so delegates that attended the conference, there were two people whom I met that day that would have a lasting influence on my academic career. The first was the Reverend Gordon Moody who has been credited with founding the Gamblers Anonymous movement in England. Until his untimely death in 1995, Gordon was someone who gave me the confidence to believe in both myself and my research into gambling.

The second person I met that day was a probation officer from south-east London called Paul Bellringer. I had invited Paul to attend our conference after coming across an article he had written about young problem gamblers. Despite our very different backgrounds we seemed to have mutual goals concerning the plight of young gamblers in the UK. Over the next year or so, our paths crossed more frequently – particularly at the meetings held by the Society for the Study of Gambling. It was at one of these meetings that Paul told me he was planning to leave his secure job in the probation service and move into the voluntary sector to form a charity which would help young problem gamblers – particularly those addicted to fruit machines. I have to admit that on first hearing this, I thought Paul was extremely brave and committed. With the job market the way it was back in the late 1980s, who in their right mind would leave a perfectly secure job to set up a charity with absolutely no guarantee of success? In retrospect, it was the right decision. Paul left his job and it was then that I realised that Paul was a man with a vision. What's more, he had a vision that I could share in, too.

Since my own doctoral research was on fruit machine addiction, I willingly accepted Paul's offer to become a Trustee of the new charity (the UK Forum on Young People and Gambling). By 1991 I had become the chair of the charity with Paul as the director. At times, the charity struggled to survive, but survive it did, and it has gone from strength to strength. The story of how this charity evolved into GamCare is told within the book by Paul himself so I won't go over that again here. However, through Paul's direction and expertise as the director of GamCare, we are continuing to see our shared vision take shape.

Some people might question why there is a need for a book such as this. Well, as someone who has been researching the psychology of gambling since 1987, I could not have predicted how fast the world of gambling would change within such a short space of time. Five years ago, I probably would not have predicted that the National Lottery or instant scratchcards would have become so integral to the British way of life and that there would be opportunities for Internet gambling, telephone betting, interactive telephone wagering and spread betting. What's more, the nature of gambling is changing. It is becoming more accessible, more technologised, and some would argue more asocial. The number of regular gamblers, and by that I mean those who gamble every single week, has increased dramatically since the introduction of the National Lottery. If we weren't a nation of gamblers in 1994, we are now! That is why a book like this is needed which takes a gambling neutral line and which takes a pragmatic and practical approach to working with problem gamblers.

There are many of us who know how hard it is to write a book on gambling and where to pitch its content. Paul was very clear on who his readership would be from the outset and has therefore written a book for practitioners from a practitioner's perspective. I very much hope that this book will become the first port of call for anyone working with problem gamblers. Paul's style is deliberately accessible and not weighed down with copious references and theoretical concerns which you might find in other writings on the subject (such as my own!). The book is comprehensible and readable and will be of direct help not only to anyone who works with problem gamblers, but also to anyone who has a problem gambler in the family or is a problem gambler themselves. I wish the book every success and I also hope that you, the reader, will feed back your own experiences and thoughts to Paul directly about the issues raised.

Preface

My first real experience of gambling was at the age of 20 when I took my mother to Cheltenham races. In my youthful arrogance I thought that all you needed was a system to make easy money from gambling. In those days Fred Winter was the champion jockey with a huge reputation. I earnestly told my mother to follow my lead and back him in every race – that way we were bound to win. She wisely abandoned my scheme after the first race when he trailed in well down the field. I persisted, however, going either for an outright win or hedging my bets with an each way result, but not once did he finish in the frame. Even in a three-horse race he came in third. When we went home after five races I did not have a single return for my betting, and was plunged into further gloom when the radio results service told me he had won the last race! At the time I felt considerably put out but looking back on it, had I won, my interest in gambling may have been from a different perspective. Early success is a common factor among those who have experienced that destructive slide from social to problem gambling.

That interest in gambling was not really rekindled until 1980 when, whilst working in the probation service, I became liaison officer for Gordon House. This facility specialised in providing residential care for offenders with a gambling problem. Although at the time I had no idea as to how much it would become part of my working life, it didn't take me long to become hooked on the social impact of gambling. The House is, in fact, named after the Reverend Gordon Moody to whom you will find several references as you read this book. I owe him a debt of gratitude as he became my mentor and helped me shape and develop an abiding interest in the social impact of gambling.

He was, in fact, the original pioneer in the development of a co-ordinated response to problem gambling in the UK. However, progress has been very slow and we are still in the process of creating a satisfactory response to both the dependency on gambling and the social impact of this deeply rooted phenomenon.

Much has been written about theories associated with gambling but this book takes a different stance in that it has been compiled with practitioners in mind. It provides information, highlights factors associated with problem gambling and outlines the more common approaches to addressing the dependency.

It sets out to assist those who wish to develop an understanding of problem gambling and those that are working, or wish to work, with this particular addiction. It is, therefore, likely to be of particular interest to practitioners who are in contact with problem gamblers and/or their families and who are engaged in encouraging them to address the dependency. Regulators, those working in the gambling industry, researchers, students and anyone with a general interest in this fascinating subject will, I hope, also find it a valuable resource.

Each chapter concludes with a summary that draws together its main theme, and a checklist that restates important points that have been raised. The first two chapters look at the role gambling plays in our society and why it is such a popular attraction. Gambling in its societal context is an obvious starting-point and, as a legal and approved leisure activity it is very appropriate also to look at the attractions of gambling. There is no doubt that as an occasional social activity gambling can rate with the best in terms of excitement and entertainment value, but the focus of the book is when that enjoyable pastime becomes problem gambling, and Chapters 3–5 explore reasons as to how and why a dependency on gambling develops. Reasons are given as to why vulnerable people find it difficult to resist deeper and deeper involvement, and how family and other factors can increase that vulnerability. Attention is paid to young problem gamblers and the differences that can be discerned between them and the older 'career' gambler.

The devastating effect of a gambling dependency comes under analysis in Chapter 6. The negative effect of problem gambling is, of course, much wider than the difficulties experienced by the gambler. It has serious and traumatic consequences for close family members, other relations, friends and work colleagues, as well as for society as a whole. Sadly, some problem gamblers spend their whole life in denial but for many a point is reached when they have had enough or when a crisis prompts them to ask for help. This is covered in Chapter 7 and is followed by a look at some of the ways that this might be encouraged. This includes a safe and relatively simple means of making that all-important first contact by ringing a telephone helpline service.

There are a number of different ways in which the problem gambler may be helped and some of the more significant approaches available in the UK are covered in Chapters 9–12. A prerequisite for any effective intervention is that of motivation; in my experience, a range of approaches are capable of encouraging change. However, I suggest that some methods are more likely to appeal to a broader section of those affected by the dependency than others. The book looks at a number of approaches and examines the principal features of various frameworks that are likely to contribute to effective intervention. As the problem does not just concern the individual, attention is also given to the family situation from the perspective both of a parent and the partner of a gambling addict.

However, the adage that 'prevention is better than cure' applies strongly to the realm of gambling. In Chapter 13 problem prevention is explored from the perspectives of legislation and regulation; the response by the gambling industry to a 'duty of care'; and the need to facilitate informed choice through awareness raising and education. Also covered in this chapter is a section on relapse prevention as helping the former problem gambler to avoid a return to dependency is as important as arresting the onset of the addiction.

It is my belief that, perhaps for the first time in many years, there is a real opportunity for society as a whole to take responsibility for the social impact of gambling, and to make adequate provision for those who are affected by a gambling dependency. Some recent developments are discussed in Chapter 14 that should help us achieve a co-ordinated and cohesive national approach to the social impact of gambling.

However, this practitioner's guide would not be complete without reference to sources of help, and there is a list of these in the final chapter. This is deliberately quite broad as it includes regulatory bodies, gambling industry associations and research centres as well as those organisations directly involved in working with problem gamblers.

In my opinion the way forward is for everyone to work together to achieve the maximisation of opportunity with the minimum of harm. This is an attainable goal if there is genuine effort on all sides to balance freedom of choice with responsibility. One strand of that is to seek a greater understanding of the problems associated with gambling and from that to develop more effective means of assisting those who are harmed by a gambling dependency. It is my hope that this book will be seen as a contribution to that objective.

1   Gambling and Society

Those two old brothers had been having a pretty hot argument a couple of days before, and had ended by agreeing to decide it by a bet, which is the English way of settling everything.

(Mark Twain, 'The £1,000,000 Bank Note')

It is my belief that we are all gamblers in one form or another. It is human nature to take risks and gambling, at its simplest, is only a stylised form of that risk taking. If this is true we can surmise that gambling has been around as long as civilisation itself. Certainly there is evidence that circa 2000 BC the Egyptians were using knuckle bones painted as four-sided dice, and 500 years later the Chinese were enjoying a recognisable form of roulette. Throughout history whether encouraged or suppressed, the need for humans to gamble has been exploited.

What is Gambling?

Perhaps it would be useful to start with a definition of gambling. Unfortunately, even this is not simple as no one seems to be able to agree as to whether speculation should be included in a definition. I am sure most dealers working the world's financial markets would deny that they are gambling but for those of us outside it certainly looks that way. In my view the sensational collapse of Barings Bank principally because of the action of one dealer is only the tip of the iceberg. However, most of us who work in this area would agree that gambling can be defined as an activity where:

- An agreement to gamble is made between two or more people.

  This may simply be two friends who bet against each other over the result of an event they are watching or a game they themselves are playing. It may also mean the transaction between a gambler and a bookmaker or other operator. In some instances, such as playing on a slot machine, the agreement between two people can be remote.

- A stake is involved which is transferred from the loser to the winner.

  Generally speaking, that stake is money but history is littered with stories where mistresses, slaves, property or land have changed hands at the turn of a card or as a result of betting on the outcome of an event. With most legalised forms of gambling a proportion of the stake and/or winnings is siphoned off as tax revenue.

- The outcome is uncertain.

  The essential central core of taking a gamble is, of course, the fact that nobody is certain of the outcome. Not only does this provide the edge of excitement in the transaction, it also exercises the human mind to rise to this challenge and devise ways of reducing that uncertainty. A whole side-industry has grown up around the desire to improve your chances of winning against all the other participants – not to mention the urge to beat the bookmaker or the casino owner.

- The result is determined (partly) by chance.

  Chance is always a factor when gambling, but for some activities the element of chance can certainly be influenced by the gambler. Take the game of blackjack, for example. This is generally seen as being a form of gaming where a skilled player can tip the chances of winning in their favour. It is a game at which a professional player can make a good living. Highly-skilled card counters also do very well but once identified by the casino are likely to find themselves excluded from the tables – it being unacceptable to the operator when the profit margin is seriously eroded by players who keep the element of chance lower than usual. On the other hand, some forms of gambling are pure chance, such as roulette or the National Lottery draw. The myriad systems employed to reduce the chance element of these activities are, I would suggest, useless.

- Participation is active.

  Whilst this might seem like a truism it is included as part of the definition because in order for the gamble to happen the participants must commit themselves to taking part. Placing the stake buys into the thrill of taking the risk and heightens the feelings associated with watching the event. Conversely, if you do not participate you cannot win.

Morality and Gambling

Despite gambling being a derivative of a natural propensity it rests uneasily with those that hold powerful positions in society. Religious faiths in particular have wrestled with gambling and, sometimes, contorted themselves into knots over the notion that it is morally wrong and evil. But because of its popularity it seems to me that exhortations not to gamble tend to be ignored by religious followers and circumvented by its leaders when advantageous to do so. The Koran, for example, expressly forbids gambling yet large numbers of Muslims can be seen at gambling venues round the world. Interestingly, the first winner of the UK National Lottery was a member of this faith. To get over this dilemma one notable cleric pragmatically decreed that Muslims can gamble when on non-Muslim territory. The Mormon church considered gambling to be morally indefensible yet was instrumental in turning Las Vegas into the gambling capital of the world. More recently in 1998 the Methodist church in England, whose stance had been to oppose gambling, has given its approval for church groups to apply for National Lottery funds.

The dichotomy experienced by religion is reflected in the history of government. In the fourteenth century gambling flourished yet in 1388 a ban was imposed on the playing of dice, quoits and tennis on a Sunday. One might suppose this was inspired by religious moralists, but in fact it had a far more pragmatic basis – King Charles II wanted to encourage soldiers to practise archery instead – one can only speculate as to whether side betting took place on the skills of the archers! Exactly 200 years later gambling was being encouraged by Elizabeth I who approved the first lottery in Britain in order to help pay for the upkeep of the Cinque Ports.

By the nineteenth century amid the growth of the Industrial Revolution, gambling in Britain was again on the increase. The first Waterloo Cup for dog racing was run in 1836, horse racing thrived and betting was commonplace. In the early part of the century casinos were illegal yet they were rife in London. Being outside the law these operated without restriction so that patrons of these gaming houses were exploited and encouraged to commit themselves way beyond their means.

In an attempt to bring casino gambling under control these gaming houses were banned by the Gaming Act of 1845. As a result their numbers began to decline, but this reduction in the opportunity to gamble in a casino was matched by a growth in List Houses. These were shops or pubs which posted the results of horse races and which were the forerunners of the modern betting shops. The concern about List Houses prompted a further Act in 1853. The Attorney-General of the day, Sir Alexander Cockburn, is quoted as saying:

> servants, apprentices, and workmen, induced by the temptation of receiving a large sum for a small one, take a few shillings to these places, and the first effect of their losing is to tempt them to go on spending their money, in the hope of retrieving their losses, and for this purpose it not infrequently happens that they are driven in to robbing their masters and employers. There is not a prison or house of correction in London which does not every day furnish abundant and conclusive testimony of the vast number of youths who are led in to crime by the temptation of these establishments. (Chin 1990)

What is interesting to me about this quote is the clear inference that the ruling class did not wish to allow widespread gambling among the working class. In this extract the Attorney-General was mostly concerned that the problem gambler would steal from the owners and so attack the established order of things.

As the century progressed the Victorians struggled with the dilemmas gambling posed and responded, by and large, in typical fashion by suppressing it. They saw it as an evil on a par with prostitution but, like the oldest profession in the world, merely succeeded in turning gambling back into a covert operation full of corruption, criminality and exploitation of the gullible.

At the beginning of the twentieth century a new gambling phenomenon reached the shores of Britain, small at the time but now the biggest money-spinner across the globe. In 1895 a San Franciscan mechanic by the name of Charles Fey produced the first slot machine which became an immediate commercial success. The three-reel machines have not changed all that much in the last 100 years although they are now driven electronically. Interestingly it has been suggested that the name 'one-armed bandit' possibly originated from these early machines that were encased in a cast iron shell. These were often given human shapes with a popular design being that of a Wild West outlaw. This bearded or masked figure had his six-gun held in an upraised left arm – which was of course the lever that set the reels in motion.

The 1906 Street Betting Act made all but betting at race meetings illegal but that did little to restrict off-course betting. Other gambling also flourished, such as hare coursing and, in the north of the country, 'tossing rings' became popular. This latter gambling activity which, under the name of 'two-up', is still popular in Australia, was a simple game that involved two coins being tossed in the air. Bets were placed as to whether they would come down two heads or two tails. If they fell one head and one tail the bet was void. Sentries were posted to watch for the police if the operators hadn't been able to 'buy' the local bobby.

Regulation of Gambling

Whilst the general policy of suppressing large-scale gambling was maintained government again looked at the possibilities of raising revenue from gambling. In 1926 Winston Churchill imposed the first betting tax. However, it was only imposed on legal on-course betting, thereby giving an immediate boost to the illegal off-course market! This farcical situation caused the tax to be abandoned three years later. After the Second World War there was a change of policy in order to tackle the extensive system of bookies' runners (bookmaker's agents) and illegal betting that had become widely acceptable and commonplace. The Betting and Gaming Act of 1960 legalised off-course betting. The same Act attempted to deal with casinos but poor drafting led to a mushrooming of exploitative and corrupt clubs. Eight years later the Gaming Act brought the situation under control and created one of the most tightly regulated casino industries in the world.

From then until 1994 the principles on which gambling was permitted in this country were that:

- Permitted forms of gambling should be available to adults subject to regulation and control so as to prevent exploitation and criminality.

- The demand for gambling should not be stimulated.

This second principle explains why few forms of gambling in this country are allowed widespread advertising and why promotional material for casinos is only just being considered (Casino Deregulation consultation paper 1998). Without doubt these principles helped restrict the spread of gambling in the UK and, together with the fear of a return to the 1960s, ensured that UK casinos are of a very different concept to their counterparts in the US and other places. It can be said

that this extremely cautious attitude towards gambling has significantly contributed to problem prevention and has helped keep the
incidence of problem gambling relatively low.

The 1990s, however, have brought a further shift of emphasis.
Increasing pressure from operators in traditional gaming markets and
the development of new betting and gaming opportunities helped
convince the government of the day that change was necessary. In
1991 a process of deregulation began which has made significant
concessions to a wide range of existing gambling in the UK. It is
without doubt, however, the introduction of the National Lottery in
November 1994 that has proved to be the catalyst to change.
Government approval of the Lottery, its widespread appeal and its very
successful operation by the licence holder Camelot all helped make it
an instant hit. But the Lottery has also been instrumental in
legitimising and popularising gambling and repositioning the activity
from a specialised to a mainstream leisure activity.

Whilst, in my view, government still wrestles with exactly where
gambling should fit in society, much of the earlier hypocrisy has
disappeared. Gone is the 'no stimulation of demand' and in its place
the government has upgraded the objectives of regulation.

The following extract from a Gaming Board report provides a good
summary as to the prevailing attitude and government thinking:

> Gambling is an activity in which the only product which changes
> hands is money. All commercial gambling is therefore cash
> generating and cash circulating and as such is susceptible to
> criminal involvement (for example through money laundering) and
> can be addictive to individuals. Excessive gambling can cause
> misery to individuals and their families. As a consequence,
> gambling is regulated in all developed countries and, whilst the
> nature of the regulatory system varies from one country to another,
> the Board believes that the following objectives are common to
> them all:
>
> – permitted forms of gambling should be crime-free (both in
>   terms of those who operate them and the players they attract),
>   conducted in accordance with regulation and honest.
>
> – players should know what to expect and be confident that they
>   will get it and should not be exploited.
>
> – there should be some protection for children and vulnerable
>   persons.
>
> Although these general principles underlie all gambling controls,

they are usually applied in different degrees to different forms of gambling. (Gaming Board for Great Britain 1997/98, p. 10)

The Betting and Gaming Act of 1960; the Betting, Gaming and Lotteries Act of 1963; and the 1968 Gaming Act, together with the Lotteries and Amusements Act of 1976, shaped modern-day regulation of the gambling industry. To this list may be added the much more recent 1993 National Lottery Act. The 1993 Act aside, this legislative framework is becoming increasingly outmoded in the face of a global growth market, the effect of modern technology on gambling activities and greater acceptability of gambling.

The Acceptability of Gambling

Whilst successive governments have taken a cautious approach in this country we now have more permissible forms of gambling than almost any other country in the world. The reason why gambling has become so acceptable is based on a combination of factors, the most salient of which include the following.

Gambling is popular. Whilst accurate figures are difficult to ascertain it is reliably suggested that prior to the introduction of the National Lottery some 69 per cent of Adults and 66 per cent of adolescents gambled. For adults this ranged from those who had a once-a-year flutter on the Grand National to the regular gambler. For adolescents this applied almost exclusively to slot machines as this was the only gambling activity to which they had legal access. Since the National Lottery has been introduced the number of 'regular' gamblers, that is once a week or more, has risen dramatically. The figure for adults who gamble has risen to 90 per cent (Mintel 1995) and adolescents to 75 per cent (Fisher 1998). The National Lottery has helped popularise and legitimise gambling and has contributed to the removal of the stigma that was formerly attached to those who gambled.

A range of gambling activities are legal. Gambling operates within a legal framework backed by regulatory authorities that have the power of inspection and control. It operates on the principle that what is not specified as legal is by definition illegal. People who wish to gamble can be reasonably sure that there is little corruption and that they are unlikely to be exploited by unscrupulous operators. Having said that, however, illegal gambling still flourishes in this country and, if some reports are to be believed, is on the increase. The largely unregulated realm of the Internet, high taxes and tight regulation has created a market for illegal betting, lotteries, other numbers games and casinos.

Gambling provides a source of government revenue. It is sometimes cynically suggested that the National Lottery was introduced as a means of raising money for the country. Furthermore, now that it has been in operation for a few years the line between government-funded projects and additional funding provided from the National Lottery good causes pot is, in the minds of many people, becoming blurred. There is no doubt that gambling is a good source of revenue and all major forms are required to pay their dues to Customs and Excise and to the Inland Revenue. In taxes and duties the latest figures suggest that £1.75 billion goes to the exchequer. If you include the money for good causes taken from National Lottery receipts a further £1.5 billion can be added (Topham and Donoughue 1998).

Gambling is big business. Despite complaints from the industry that the regulations are too stringent, that the tax burden is too high and that some activities get more favourable treatment than others, gambling is a growth industry both in the UK and on a global scale. Again quoting from Topham and Donoughue's 1998 report on the UK gaming industry the total turnover of gambling, that is the amount staked, for 1996 was £40 billion. That equates to a staggering average of £110 million being staked on gambling every day of the year. If you include illegal gambling and the probability that slot machine turnover has been under-reported the real figure could be in excess of £135 million a day. Of course, much of this money transaction is circular in that it is returned in winnings and then gambled again. The actual spend is calculated as being in the region of £7 billion which works out as £19 million a day. Whichever way it is looked at the betting and gaming business is a significant industry. It directly employs thousands of people and indirectly sustains many thousands more through catering, supplies of goods, and by helping to support companies where gambling forms the profitable aspect of a wider business. It must also be recognised that gambling companies are great supporters of sports events and, in the case of the horse racing industry, help keep this going through a government-imposed betting levy. The larger operators are also generous contributors to charity either through their own organisation, such as the Camelot Foundation, or by direct support to a selected charity, such as Ladbroke Racing's recent support for SCOPE (formerly the Spastics Society).

The Availability of Gambling

In the space of a few years the availability of gambling has greatly increased. Traditional forms of gambling, such as the betting office, are, since deregulation in the 1990s, far more attractive places to visit and have taken a greater prominence on the high street. New arrivals, most notably the National Lottery, have inhabited hitherto 'gambling free' zones and like slot machines break the mould of containing gambling within specific designated venues. Gambling is also increasingly available without ever having to set foot outside your front door.

If you are looking for a gambling venue and take a walk down the local high street, you are likely to find any or all of the following attractions on offer:

- A **casino**, where once you have registered as a member you can chance your luck 24 hours later by playing roulette, card games, dice or high-payout slot machines.

- One or more **betting offices** (bookies) attractively designed to encourage betting on the horses, the dogs (greyhound racing), a set of numbers, sporting events, elections, the weather and much more besides. You can also participate in a society lottery and, since 1996, you have been able to gamble in the betting office on relatively low-payout slot machines.

- The local **bingo club** providing a social gambling environment to play endless games of bingo and take part in a daily national game offering a jackpot of £500,000. The club additionally offers another opportunity to play the slot machines, either those with a low payout or a smaller number offering a higher return.

- An **amusement arcade** may well be sited a few doors further on offering a whole range of electronic entertainment including gaming machines with a range of relatively low payouts.

But, you do not have to seek out a specific venue that caters for gambling as there are many other opportunities on offer on the high street:

- The **corner shop, supermarket or post office** is likely to offer lottery tickets, scratchcards and the chance to purchase football pools coupons.

- The **cafe** may well sport a couple of fruit machines beckoning enticingly from the corner.

- Almost every **pub** includes among the amenities on offer one or two fruit machines to play as you sip your pint. You can also buy scratchcards or football pools coupons. For a short while some pubs also offered an on-line draw game and there has been some experimentation with selling National Lottery tickets.

- The **newsagent** might not only have a Lottery terminal and scratchcard display but is likely to sell newspapers with scratchcards enclosed or which offer the chance to take part in some gambling-related competition.

- **Railway or bus stations**. If you have got this far without succumbing to the exhortation to gamble, chances are that there will be more machines encouraging you to take a chance with your loose change.

- Other premises, such as **cinemas** and **leisure centres**, are also likely to have a couple of fruit machines available.

Away from the main shopping area further opportunities to gamble beckon:

- A trip to the **racecourse** is for many people an enjoyable and entertaining day out and for almost everyone who goes part of the excitement is in placing a bet with the on-course bookmaker or the Tote.

- An evening at **the dogs** provides an added attraction for some, especially as you can place your bet and watch the greyhounds without leaving your place at the dinner table.

- **Sporting events** allow further opportunities to bet on the outcome so adding spice to your enjoyment of the football match, Formula One race, or alternative contest of skill and courage.

- Other venues, such as **motorway service areas, theme parks** and **fairgrounds** will almost certainly have a section of amusements that will probably include gambling machines.

If your desire to gamble has not abated when you arrive home further chances to risk your money are available:

- **Agents** may call at the door to sell and to collect football pool coupons.

- **Telephone betting** is available to those who have obtained clearance to open an account with their favourite bookmaker. It operates in similar fashion to placing a bet in the shop but from the comfort of your armchair.

- **Spread betting,** which has for some time been confined to those involved with the financial markets, is beginning to gain popularity. This more complex form of betting allows you to gamble by pitting your judgement against that of the firm that offers a spread against any particular event or outcome. Like telephone betting, financial clearance is a prerequisite for taking part.

- The **Internet** already has hundreds of gambling sites available to those who are prepared to commit their credit card details to the (mainly off-shore) operators. As nearly all these sites are outside the jurisdiction of the UK they are not subject to UK laws, regulation or control. Nevertheless, Internet gambling is an increasing attraction to many who surf the web.

- **Interactive television** hitherto restricted to consoles on the back of aircraft seats, will provide further opportunity to gamble at home now that digital television is available.

It is quite remarkable that in such a short space of time gambling has been catapulted from an activity that you had to seek out to one that appears to be available everywhere. The decision process has changed from consciously deciding to gamble to that of deciding not to gamble. For instance, I have been told by people who don't buy a lottery ticket that they have a strong sense of being a minority group, and of being looked upon as being slightly odd. One possible explanation for this extraordinary change is that many people who do buy lottery tickets do not see it as a form of gambling. They cling to the belief, articulated by the government Heritage Minister in 1994, that it is a 'harmless flutter'. In my mind, however, there is no doubt that the introduction of the National Lottery proved to be a catalyst for change and paved the way for an age of the gambling 'emporium'. This shift in emphasis and acceptance of gambling has far-reaching implications for society.

Gambling and the Future

The move away from the previously hypocritical and highly ambivalent attitude to gambling is, in my opinion, a healthy step forward. It is also timely as the traditional method of regulating gambling is under serious challenge from modern technology and methods of communication. Gambling is, without doubt, a global growth industry. Whilst people will always wish to go out to be entertained, they can increasingly amuse themselves at home by logging on to the

Internet and with the advent of digital television will be able to interact through this medium. There are already a large number of gambling web sites available and this type of activity seems to be a natural choice for interactive television.

The opportunity and, I would suggest, the encouragement to gamble are likely to increase. It is therefore vitally important that we as a society decide how much we wish gambling to become part of our culture and the extent to which it should be readily available. The responsibility for this lies not only with government but with the gambling industry, those organisations that concern themselves with social impact issues and with everyone who gambles. Controlled gambling is a fun, exciting form of entertainment that brings a number of positive benefits to society. Uncontrolled gambling is destructive to society as a whole as much as it is to the individual.

SUMMARY

Gambling is a stylised form of risk taking that has a number of definable factors. It is an activity that has caused controversy for centuries and governments world-wide have alternately suppressed or encouraged its growth. Even when gambling has been allowed the need for strong regulation has usually been recognised. In the UK gambling has become increasingly acceptable and in tandem with this attitude is now widely available. This process of change has accelerated in the last few years with the majority of the adult population now gambling on a regular basis.

CHECKLIST

Gambling is a stylised form of risk taking which may be classified under the following definitions:

- An agreement to gamble is made by two or more people.
- The stake is transferred from loser to winner.
- The outcome is uncertain.
- The result is determined, partly, by chance.
- Participation is active.

The opportunity to gamble has increased hugely within the last few years. Principal reasons for this acceptability are because it is:

- Popular – over 90 per cent of adults gamble to some extent.
- Legal – a wide range of gambling activities are permissible in the UK.
- A source of government revenue – approaching £2 bn in tax and duty.
- Big business – turnover is in excess of £40 bn per annum.

Gambling has become much more widely available and this access is likely to increase further. The places where gambling activities are on offer include:

- casinos
- bingo clubs
- other clubs
- amusement arcades
- cafes and fish and chip shops
- corner shops, supermarkets and post offices
- betting offices
- pubs
- bus and railway stations, airports and ferry terminals
- motorway service stations
- newsagents
- through door-to-door sales and collections
- the racecourse
- the dog track
- sports events
- over the telephone
- on the Internet

2 The Attractions of Gambling

A love affair with Lady Luck.

(anonymous gambler)

It is in our very nature to take a risk, part of our approach to life. We all take risks every day; for example, in choosing what to eat or what to wear; in our conversations; in the actions we take; in how we manage our money; in making, holding and breaking relationships. Risk taking permeates thinking, feeling and emotions to give us a chance, hope, a sense of being alive. Without the ability to assess an opportunity or respond to a threat we would wither or die.

As I established in the previous chapter, gambling is a stylised form that meets basic human needs. Gambling can give you a sense of belonging, a status, a feeling of achievement. Just carrying through the activity of gambling can make you feel good – being on the edge, doing something daring, committing yourself to fate, or pitting yourself against the odds. When that dare comes off and you win, the feel good factor is magnified, the fact that you are special is endorsed.

> I started playing fruit machines at 15, I used to play in cafes, I remember the first time I played, I put in 20p and won £1. I was dead chuffed. (Paul – college student aged 18)

When gamblers are asked what the experience of gambling equates to they are often hard pressed to draw a parallel. A group of gamblers in prison responded to the question 'What other experience comes nearest to gambling?' by unanimously saying 'Being on the job' – the act of committing a crime (Moody 1994). A very small group of adolescent fruit machine addicts were recorded as describing sexual intercourse as the nearest equivalent pleasurable experience to the 'high' they felt when playing (Griffiths 1995).

Why is Gambling Attractive?

Taking a look at the activity of gambling itself, a number of reasons as to why it becomes attractive have been suggested by a range of researchers. The following are the most significant reasons:

Gambling is a form of play

It is often suggested that gambling is essentially a form of play and, as such, is inescapably interwoven into the natural culture of both child and adult (Callois 1962, Abt and Smith 1984, Browne 1989). So, if it is a form of play it can be seen as the opposite of work and as such may be viewed as the attraction of pleasure seeking (Devereux 1949). I recall talking to a former professional blackjack player who stated that he had given it all up because when he started to gamble as a means of earning his living it ceased to be fun and became work.

It is this element of fun that is quoted time and again by gamblers as a main attraction. We are not talking of the passive fun that can be had from watching a good show, but fun coupled with excitement that comes from participation. Whilst gambling can, unfortunately, become a lonely occupation for those that become dependent, for those that keep it within the bounds of a social activity the fun is enhanced when in the company of friends. Gambling with others can act as a spur to be even more daring or, conversely, as a restraint – to go easy and not to chase losses.

Play is also significant in the marketing of gambling as it is heavily promoted as a leisure activity. For example, lottery tickets are called 'playslips', people 'play' on a machine, potential participants are invited to 'play' a game of cards, and so on.

Gambling provides entertainment

Whilst there are several reasons why controlled gambling has beneficial effects in a society, none of these are essential. Gambling is a form of entertainment which, depending on the activity, may rely purely on chance or might have an element of skill that can be brought to bear to improve the chances of winning. The most appropriate way of looking at gambling is to keep in mind that you are simply buying entertainment and, if you win, it is a bonus. Paying the stake is the entrance fee to being entertained, to enjoying your performance and, in environments such as the casino, enjoying watching or participating in the drama of the gaming tables.

This link with entertainment can be seen in a wider context. Take the Grand National, for instance. This annual spectacle creates enormous interest in the UK; not just because it is one of the toughest horse races in the sporting calendar but also because millions of people see it as an event for which they have paid (by placing a bet) to watch. The draw for the National Lottery occupies a slot on prime-time television that not only builds up the glitz and glamour of gambling but also promotes the artists who present and support the draw.

Opportunities to gamble are widely available

Only 20 years ago you had to seek out the opportunities to gamble and, if you were a recovering problem gambler, routing your journey to avoid gambling venues was a very real safety strategy. The situation is vastly different now as it is possible to walk down a street in the UK and be confronted with a whole range of gambling activities (see Chapter 1).

However, gambling is not confined to the high street – on the edge of many towns you might be able to see a few of the 7500 horse races that take place each year, or visit one of the 32 registered dog tracks.

Increasingly, if you so choose you do not even have to leave the confines of your own home to be able to gamble twenty-four hours a day. You mind find a scratchcard with your morning paper, have an account with your favourite bookmaker, or be cleared to indulge in a financial market crossover with gambling known as spread betting.

Switching on your computer and logging on to the websites will reveal several hundred opportunities to gamble by using your credit card which, in most UK-regulated activities, is not permissible.

We are therefore presented with vast opportunities to gamble as its availability impinges more and more on our everyday lives. This greater availability is likely to result in more people gambling more often. This can ably be illustrated by the increase from 69 per cent to 90 per cent in the number of adults who gamble in the UK following the introduction of the National Lottery (Mintel 1995).

Gambling offers a chance to win money

Money plays a very significant role in the activity of gambling. You might consider this to be stating the obvious but in fact the role of money is not simply that of winning. Primarily money provides the means of participating or continuing to participate in the gambling activity.

Whilst many people, especially young teenagers, express their reason for gambling as a means of winning money, this can be considered a rational justification.

> The hardest thing for non-gamblers to understand, it seems to me, is that money loses its economic value in gambling .... In the casinos, the transformation of money into coloured counters, children's play-things, into a part of the game itself, serves to weaken the player's natural instinct .... The only time you notice money, as world cham-pion Doyle Brunson has said, is when you put your hand in your pocket and find it empty. (Spanier 1987, p. 142)

The use of chips in a casino or tokens to play a fruit machine therefore helps divorce the fact that you are spending money from participating in the activity. The slot machine industry is keen to move away from the regulation that ties the playing of slots to use of 'a coin of the realm'. The advent of electronic payment devices will be another means by which money is divorced from the act of participation.

Goods of equivalent monetary value can be exchanged for tokens won from playing Amusement With Prizes machines (low-payout slot machines). These aside, gambling payouts are usually equated with money. The act of winning is emphasised in many gambling activities. For example, it is no coincidence that slot machine payout trays have traditionally been made of metal to increase the sound of a win. National Lottery jackpot amounts and winners who are brave or foolhardy enough to be identified are hyped up in the media.

> Have thousands of chances to win millions of dollars by playing the lotteries the 'smart way'! Don't delay – win big today! (Internet advertisement 1998)

Having said that the role of money is primarily the means to participate in gambling, the amount that can be won and the thrill experienced when there is only a small gain is still significant. The chance of winning a huge amount for a small stake is known to provide a big incentive for someone to begin to gamble. The fact that over 60 per cent of adults in the UK regularly buy a lottery ticket illustrates the attraction of the big win, despite the fact that the odds are 14 million to 1. On the other hand occasional social gamblers can get very excited when their £2 stake on the 2-1 favourite, Flying Fred, wins at Ascot.

Gambling is a part of culture

There is no doubt that gambling is part of the culture in Britain and has been for a very long time. The first recorded horse race took place in AD 210 (TACADE 1992) and it is reasonable to assume that there was some form of bet on the outcome. Lotteries have been periodically approved in order to raise money for specific purposes – the first in Britain being that of 1588 in order to help pay for the repair of the Cinque Ports. The UK has been home to many ethnic groups, such as the Jews and the Chinese who have brought their love of gambling with them.

Horse racing has been known as the Sport of Kings and there are many stories of the fortunes won or lost by members of the aristocracy in the last 200 years. For lesser mortals, dog racing and betting on the outcome, one can surmise, has been going on for hundreds of years.

Over time, the nation's love affair with gambling has waxed and waned but even when it was suppressed illegal gambling has proliferated. A good example of this is the situation that prevailed in the 1950s when off-course betting was illegal. At that time bookies' runners could be sought out on street corners, in the workplace or at the local pub. In many instances police were bought off, or actually took part in the process of illegal betting. Recognising the sheer popularity of betting, and wanting to kill off the growing racketeering and crime associated with illegal betting, the government paved the way for the high street betting office in its 1960 Betting and Gaming Act.

Gambling terminology is part of everyday language: 'I bet that it will rain today', 'What're the odds', 'Bingo! There it was', 'Holding all the cards'. Casino gambling and betting have added richness to the language for many years. The phrase 'I bet' is common in some circles as a means of reinforcing, or simply stating, an opinion. More recently the expression of desired acquisition is often preceded by 'If I win the lottery I'll ...'.

Dice, cards and 'pitch and toss' have provided entertainment, amusement and angst for centuries. Before the introduction of television, card games provided a popular family pastime. I can personally remember Gran's button box being used to provide the means of the stake to play 'Newmarket'. The point being of course that even at that innocent level the concept of gambling was being instilled, and, despite national prohibition, small-scale gambling was part of everyday life.

More recently gambling has become a stronger thread in the lives and affairs of the nation. Wider share ownership and the huge speculative risks transacted daily on the stock market are indicative of how important gambling is in the micro and macro economy. This shift towards greater participation has been developing for decades. The process of opening up modern gambling to the whole population began in the 1960s with acts concerning betting and with the increasing number of casinos. The 1980s witnessed the growth of slot machines and the 1990s heralded the advent of the National Lottery. The cumulative effect of increasing the range of legal gambling activities and encouragement to participate has removed the stigma that publicly attached itself to gambling and has turned it into an almost universally approved activity. With the advance of electronics and growth of telecommunications this cultural acceptance of gambling is set to become even more prominent in the lives of the majority.

Gambling provides action

One of the most magnetically attractive aspects of gambling is the feelings experienced by participating in the activity.

The enjoyment of the 'action' is enjoyment of taking risk after risk in rapid and continuous succession, and risk really means risk – you catch your breath when you realise what is at stake. (Moody 1990, p. 21)

First, there is the anticipation – and this can begin long before the gambler arrives at the venue. Thoughts about gambling, taking a risk, being lucky can create a little frisson of pleasure. The point of arrival provides a boost to the pleasure. Walking into the arcade, betting office or casino can induce a tingle of anticipation.

Having arrived at the slot machine, betting shop counter or blackjack table, the tension begins to mount as the point at which you are going to commit yourself to taking the risk beckons you forward. Paying the stake is the commitment and then that tension is held during the activity. Studies of roulette players have recorded a doubling of heart rate whilst the ball is spinning round the wheel. You feel good, you are committed, you are doing it, the game is on. Are you going to win?

The game ends, the result is known; win or lose, the tension begins to ebb away to be replaced by feelings of joy and elation if you have won, by a thrill if you nearly won, and by disappointment assuaged by hope for the next bet when you lose. The intensity of these feelings can be affected by a number of factors:

- *How long you have been playing*: The build-up and release of tension is likely to be less after playing for a while than at the beginning, unless the importance of winning is such that a high intensity is maintained.

- *The value of nearly winning*: Psychological studies suggest that the buzz experienced from a near miss is nearly as great as that obtained from winning. Heavy gamblers interpret this as nearly winning and are likely to continue playing in the expectation of an actual win even though, in reality, they are persistently losing (Griffiths 1995).

- *How many times you have won or lost during the session*: If you lose consistently, the importance of a win increases and so the tension associated with each subsequent game is likely to remain high. How close you are to quitting can also be a factor as reaching an expenditure limit or exhausting your credit may heighten feelings.

- *How much you have staked on the outcome*: For many gamblers the amount staked would have a bearing on the tension experienced – particularly when a regular pattern is broken and a larger stake is wagered, thereby increasing the risk.

- *How important it is for you to win*: If a sense of competition against other players or against the gamble itself is present, or if there is a strong need for ego-enhancement in your play, or the payout is very important to you, it is likely that a high level of tension will be maintained.

> Goffman suggests that it is the voluntary submission to the activity that specifically provides the thrill and excitement which he calls action. Whilst the gambler is strongly attracted to the thrill this state of tension imparts he also finds it intolerable and seeks ways of easing it. One of these is the repression of emotions so as to deaden feelings about the event. This has particular significance as it lends weight to the theory as to why males seek action in gambling. The maintenance of self discipline in the face of barely tolerable tension can reap a reward more highly prized than money – the gain of kudos and approval amongst the gambler's peer group. (Bellringer and Fisher 1997, p. 31)

The high-frequency gambling activities are the ones that provide the greatest opportunities to feel good by continuing the action. With a fruit machine, for example, the reels only spin for five seconds, so, if the feature buttons are not pressed, the build-up and release of tension can be repeated in a very short time-span. Throw in the manipulation of the buttons, the near-misses and the actual wins and you have a very powerful interactive form of gambling that induces a strong desire to experience the thrill again and again.

Gambling provides an escape

The act of gambling coupled to the environment meets a human need and provides a powerful escape from reality. It can take you to a fantasy world in which you can feel powerful and cast off all the negative feelings of everyday life.

> The experience [of gambling] provides a door to a magical new world. It is amazing: there you are, engrossed at a gaming table, in a betting office or face-to-face with a gaming machine, lost to all the world. From the outside it looks so cramping, so limited, but you are experiencing the magic of Dr Who's Tardis. For the person who is in on the 'action' it is like the whole universe, bright with stars and full of wonder. (Moody 1990, p. 21)

The mental concentration required in the participation, coupled with a feeling of power in this fantasy world takes the gambler away from thinking about life outside. The greater the pressure in their life the greater the relief when they are actually gambling. Feelings of inadequacy disappear, for although the outcome is uncertain, it is equally uncertain for whoever plays. This equality of chance is a great comfort, different from the unfair world outside, and can be enhanced in an environment such as a casino where you can feel equal to people who are beyond your social group. Being able to play in these conditions restores a sense of empowerment and of being transported to a comfortable place where you are valued.

Gambling is a form of problem solving

The problem-solving process involved in many gambling activities, and the need to beat the system, can be particularly attractive to some gamblers. Studying the horses, for example, has become a science. Books are written about it, there are clubs you can join that provide reams of information, and many punters spend hours checking facts, figures, opinions and gut reactions. With horse racing there is undoubtedly an element of skill in making a selection, so such attention to detail may increase a gambler's return. When it comes to systems for the National Lottery or for roulette, as games of pure chance, working out the possibilities is not going to make any difference – but it might make the gambler feel better by providing an illusion of control. Therefore, it should be recognised that a need is being met in the studying and ritual associated with gambling activities.

I have already identified that gambling can provide a feeling of being in control. As long as the gambler has the means to continue the activity, that good feeling can be maintained. When gamblers win there is a deep feeling of satisfaction that their problem-solving approach has paid off and they have overcome the system. This is of particular significance to those gamblers who feel disempowered elsewhere in their lives. Here is an opportunity to be in control of their own destiny, to make and act on decisions, to feel skilful.

Some gambling activities feed into this need to feel in control – slot machines with feature buttons to delay spinning, to move individual reels, and so on, provide an illusion of control that many young gamblers cite as the principal reason for playing.

> I believed I had the skill to win more. I felt in command like some starship pilot, pushing buttons to manoeuvre the [fruit] machine where I wanted it to go, what I wanted it to do. (Problem gambler – soldier, aged 19)

Gambling environments are attractive

It is no accident that many gambling environments cocoon and shelter the gambler from the outside world. They are deliberately designed to help people escape from the reality of their everyday lives.

In a casino, for example, time is suspended as you are unlikely to find a clock, the gaming floor will probably have no windows or the curtains are kept drawn, and lighting levels are generally kept low. The decor may well be red to stimulate and to induce a sense of excitement, mixed with blue to create a sense of peace and security.

By way of contrast the amusement arcade is usually a brash, noisy place but just as seductive to the clientele that it wants to attract. Many young gamblers talk about the 'brilliant' atmosphere to be found in an arcade. The loud music, sound effects from individual machines and flashing lights help create an aura of excitement and fun that strikes a responsive chord in young people. The arcade is seen as a meeting place, a focal point, a cultural space for young people of both sexes, and its appeal is increased by the fact that it is an environment disapproved of and shunned by many adults. The fact that the arcade is relatively free from adult supervision and control is a bonus for the clientele. Interestingly this poses a dilemma for many arcade operators who want to attract young people but find that often, and particularly so in the case of younger teenagers, they spend relatively little money yet cause most of the disruption and problems.

However, if you visited some of those arcades in the daytime the environment may well have changed. The music would be softer, the flashing lights muted and the atmosphere would have a different social feel to it. This is an altogether more attractive scene for the older women who find solace and pleasure in the arcade and in playing the more straightforward slot machines.

The betting office used to have a similar reputation for being a closed world frequented mostly by men who were often seen as being 'somewhat disreputable' by those who didn't bet or disapproved of the activity. The spartan and very masculine interior of those betting shops was largely induced by government regulations that demanded austerity and that the inside remain hidden from public view. Deregulation in 1993 heralded a major change of policy by allowing clear frontage, improved refreshment facilities, larger television screens and greater comfort. This has led the way for the industry to attract a broader customer base into the bookmaker.

For all these improvements the betting office cannot match the spectacle and colour of the race track. A day out at the races is still seen as an occasion enjoyed by thousands. Courses like Aintree, Ascot and Epsom have special significance in the sporting calendar and attract huge interest as the nation gets caught up in the excitement and the atmosphere.

Quite apart from the attraction of gambling to the players this activity is seen by governments throughout the world as a means of boosting revenue and, in many jurisdictions, providing money for projects that would otherwise founder for lack of cash. As discussed in Chapter 1, the money that can be gained from gambling provides a strong attraction for governments as well as individuals.

Obviously, gambling is also seen as attractive to the companies that run the various activities. Despite heavy rates of taxation and restraints on trade, there are healthy profits to be made. In the UK, piecemeal legislation has created a situation whereby the different forms of gambling compete with one another for market share. Consequently, any change in the legislation is likely to have a beneficial effect on part of the market to the detriment of another activity. For example, the marketing advantage given to the National Lottery when it was introduced in 1994 depressed the football pools market and saw a reduction in betting turnover.

Despite these pressures the gaming industry is thriving and is seen by the operators as providing a necessary and worthwhile service.

> The company is keen to help communities where our premises are situated, and it also supports local and national charities. ... In this way our company can be seen to be playing a reasonable role in both the wider and local communities from which we earn our income ... we provide safe employment for 3,100 people ... we contribute massively to the exchequer ... and we support many local businesses ... Many people think there is something wrong with gambling. They believe there is a weakness in the character of a person who likes a bet. They are wrong, narrow minded and short sighted in that moderate gambling gives a great deal of pleasure to a great many people, while the cost factor is small. (L. Steinberg 1993, p. 2)

SUMMARY

Gambling is an attractive activity for the great majority of the population in the UK. We gamble for a variety of reasons that generate good feelings related to risk taking, active participation, escapism, problem solving and an attractive environment. Despite an ambivalence in society as to the extent to which gambling should be allowed, the UK has in the 1990s witnessed its legitimisation. Opportunities to gamble are increasing and it is widely available. This growth of gambling is sanctioned by government which benefits by a significant contribution in revenue and the feel good factor. It is an attractive business which, when effectively run and competitively well placed, can generate a good return and contribute positively to the leisure industry.

CHECKLIST

Gambling is a stylised form of risk taking that meets a number of human needs. Gambling is an attractive activity because it is:

- **A form of play** that is part of the culture of both children and adults.

- **Entertaining** and nowadays seen as an acceptable part of the leisure industry.

- **Easily available** as a whole range of gambling activities can be found on the high street.

- **Possible to win money** although the role of money is that of being able to carry through the decision to gamble.

- **Part of the culture** of both the indigenous population and ethnic minorities..

- **An exciting action** that is linked to the build-up and release of tension and heightened by the risk of losing the stake.

- **A means of escape** into a fantasy world that can relieve, or block out, pressures and problems of everyday life.

- **A challenge** that provides a chance of overcoming the odds, of foretelling the future, and of coming out on top.

- **A problem-solving activity** that for many becomes an important factor in the process of taking a gamble.

- **A social activity** that is often located in an environment that people are drawn to and like.

- **Meeting a desire for control** which, despite being transitory can be significant for some gamblers.

- **Certain of providing an outcome** that, with most gambling activities, becomes known within a relatively short period of time.

3   How Gambling Becomes a Problem

I had found a dream world into which I could escape.

(Charlie – former shop manager, aged 44)

For most people gambling does not dominate their lives; it is an occasional or regular activity that provides a spot of entertainment, the thrill of taking a chance, and the hope of a win. Whether it is watching the horses at the race track, studying form in the bookies, buying a lottery ticket or ticking off the numbers at the bingo club, it provides the social gambler with pleasure and gives a lift to the routine of the day.

A day at the races or a night at the casino can be a special occasion that is the high spot of a celebration or a few hours of good entertainment. The enjoyment of gambling is enhanced by its sociability: getting involved in the action among friends, enjoying the ups and downs in fortune of your group, feeling secure in collective risk taking and providing a memorable talking-point to look back on can be the pay-off for many occasional gamblers.

For the regular gamblers the daily bet on the horses, playing the pub slot machine, or a Wednesday night at bingo provides a cheerful strand of their lifestyle. The anticipation of the forthcoming event, leaving behind worldly cares, meeting friends at the venue, experiencing the excitement when taking part, and reflecting on the results afterwards all contribute to the appeal of social gambling.

For a number of gamblers, however, what begins as a social activity touches a core need and triggers a craving that becomes increasingly hard to resist.

> The action makes you feel good. You must go back and get more. For a while, the innocence and purity remain untouched. All too soon, however, gambling begins to trespass onto areas of your life where it has no place to be. (Moody 1990, p. 22)

What is Problem Gambling?

Whilst it may have a different starting-point for each individual it can be said that gambling becomes a problem when, as a result of the activity, it creates serious adverse consequences for the individual or for others with whom the gambler is associated. Many different words are used to describe the adverse consequences of gambling and a number of those are used in this book. 'Pathological gambling' is one commonly-used term to describe those at the extreme end of the continuum. This has been recognised by the World Health Organization (WHO) in its classification of Mental and Behavioural Disorders:

> The disorder consists of frequent, repeated episodes of gambling which dominate the individual's life to the detriment of social, occupational, material, and family values and commitments. Those who suffer from this disorder may put their jobs at risk, acquire large debts, and lie or break the law to obtain money or evade payment of debts. They describe an intense urge to gamble, which is difficult to control, together with a preoccupation with ideas and images of the act of gambling and the circumstances that surround the act. These preoccupations and urges often increase at times when life is stressful. (WHO 1995)

At the other end of the scale social gamblers may occasionally commit more resources than they can afford which creates difficulties elsewhere in their life. The generic name recognised internationally to describe someone who is experiencing adverse affects of gambling is that of 'problem gambler'.

Signs and Symptoms of Problem Gambling

For some the descent from social to problem gambling happens very quickly. For others it is a more gradual process as the feel good factor to be got from gambling is not matched by anything else.

Gambling is often referred to as the 'hidden addiction' because unlike other dependencies it is much more difficult to identify when someone's gambling is out of control. Some of the reasons for this are:

- there are no physical symptoms as there are with, for instance, drug use or alcoholism
- money shortages and debts can be explained away with ease in a materialistic society
- gamblers do not believe they have a problem or wish to hide the fact
- gamblers unaffected by drink or drugs are exceedingly plausible and become adept at lying to mask the truth

- young problem gamblers making the transition from child- to adulthood may be experiencing several excessive behaviours.

Additionally, the signs and symptoms are, in many instances, similar to those that are exhibited with other dependencies. It is, therefore, easy to attribute the reason for a gambler's behaviour to some other cause, and it cannot be overlooked that an individual's pattern of behaviour may be symptomatic of more than one dependency.

However, a cluster of possible symptoms would provide a good indication that a person's gambling has moved from being a social activity to that of being a problem. The following are some of the more common symptoms:

The gambler is spending too much money on gambling. This clearly has a relative value in that the determinant is how much the individual can afford to spend on gambling. For an unemployed person with no savings or other financial means £1 a week may be too much, but for the person with a high disposable income and few commitments the figure could be thousands of pounds. Regardless of the figure involved it becomes a problem when the activity takes up more financial resources than the gambler can afford to lose.

The gambler is spending too much time gambling. This again is relative to the life of the individual but there is clearly a problem when time spent gambling is making inroads into obligations towards college, work, social life, personal relationships or family.

Gambling is seen as a legitimate means of making money. It is true that a few 'professional' gamblers can and do make their money out of the activity, but the majority of those who gamble may occasionally win, will sometimes break even but are more likely to finish up out of pocket. The operator of the activity in not a philanthropist and will usually exclude a gambler who is able to win consistently. Nevertheless, problem gamblers and many young social gamblers naively think that gambling is a legitimate means of making money.

> I had to play the machines. I could not resist their lure, their promise of easy money. But their lure and promise made life an awful lot more miserable than it is meant to be. (Gary – unemployed, aged 22)

Chasing losses. This is a hallmark of a problem gambler. Anyone who frequently exceeds their original self-imposed limit, or who has to replenish their supply of money in order to try and recoup what has been lost, is sliding inexorably towards the problem end of the gambling continuum. High-frequency games such as slot machines or scratchcards can, by the rapidity and interaction of the play, tempt the gambler into chasing after money already spent.

Gambling alone for long periods. As individuals move from being social to problem gamblers they become reluctant to gamble in the company of their family or friends. Alternatively, they might begin a session with companions but are likely to continue long after their friends have moved on to do something else. As the problem progresses, relationships suffer and it becomes less likely that a partner or companion will encourage the gambler. The company they keep gravitates towards other heavy and excessive gamblers or they become isolated within their preferred gambling environment.

Persuading others to gamble. The need for self-justification prompts a number of problem gamblers to persuade their friends and colleagues to gamble with them. This persuasion is, however, likely to be selective in order to hide the extent of gambling from some people – particularly those to whom they owe money.

Borrowing money. As problem gambling develops, more and more money is needed to satisfy the craving. Gamblers will, in the first instance, use up all of their own resources. They will then approach friends and family to borrow money. Should they experience a big win they might pay off these debts but they will soon reappear. Requests to pay back what has been borrowed are repelled with plausible stories of financial bad luck and renewed promises to return the loan with interest.

Selling personal possessions. The need for more money than they have at their command causes problem gamblers to sell their own personal possessions. This frequently extends to any item bought on a hire purchase agreement, but the money realised from the sale is spent on further gambling and the debt remains unpaid. Family possessions are also likely to be sold, the disappearance of which being disguised by the gambler faking a burglary or by concocting some totally false story.

Criminal activity. As the situation spirals further out of control and the pressure to repay debts increases many problem gamblers step over the threshold into criminal activity. Those crimes that provide instant cash or where money is readily obtained from the process of crime are most favoured by the gambler in trouble.

Because of the erroneous belief that the next bet will produce a win big enough to repay everyone problem gamblers may not even believe that they have committed theft – they may see it merely as having borrowed the money temporarily as a means of getting more.

Having been encouraged to gamble when young. When talking to problem gamblers many say their first experience was whilst on holiday with their parents. They were given a sum of money and told to go off and play in the arcade for a while. Gambling being an approved activity in the family is another significant sign, either because a parent or relation had been a heavy gambler or because gambling took place within the family group.

> My gambling started when I was six playing card games with my parents and other members of the family. I found out later that they often let me win which led me to believe I was good at this, I could beat the grown-ups. (Problem gambler, cited in *New Life* 1995)

The gambling environment is part of a lifestyle. As the activity moves from being an occasional social pastime to an all-consuming passion the gamblers' whole lifestyle becomes centred around the need to gamble. They are likely to become very knowledgeable about their preferred activity and if prompted may readily talk animatedly about it. They will spend hours of their week in the amusement arcade, betting office or casino. Whilst some may gamble only on a single activity, as the search for 'action' intensifies, problem gamblers may well develop a liking for several activities. Their day could well start by studying racing form in the newspaper prior to spending the afternoon in the bookies. From there it is off to the dog track for the evening and, if they still have money to spend, on to the casino until the early hours of the morning. These gamblers are unlikely to go home with any money.

Blind optimism. Many problem gamblers articulate a sense of optimism about their future even when it is quite unrealistic. That need to believe that they are special leads them to think that a combination of luck and skill will transform their situation for the better. Therefore long-term plans might well have a touch of the fantastical. It is more likely, however, that their focus will be on the 'here and now', looking for short-term solutions to cover the immediate difficulties that are besetting them.

Who is Vulnerable?

Problem gambling is no respecter of age, social group or intelligence. It can and does affect people from all walks of life. There are a number of theories as to why a dependency on gambling develops and why some people are more vulnerable than others. In my view the diversity of these theories and of research findings suggest that the reasons are a complex mix of psychological, biological and sociological factors. The individual characteristics of a gambler (personality, attitudes, beliefs, and so on), the wide range of variable external influences (such as external environment, accessibility to gambling, advertising) and the nature of the gambling activity itself (for example, size of the jackpot, payout structure and event frequency) are likely to be the determinants as to whether gambling moves from a social to a problem activity. There are, however, a number of factors that are commonly associated with problem gambling.

The gambler feels inferior to peer group and elders. This feeling of inferiority usually begins early in the gambler's life and is reinforced by later experiences. Gambling is a means of being seen to be superior whether the gambler wins or loses. When they win gamblers can give the appearance of being more successful than both the one who is losing and the non-gambler who has not had the 'courage' to take part. When they lose, kudos can be retained by maintaining a nonchalant and 'cool' attitude, as if it doesn't matter. As they become more secretive, however, gamblers would normally keep very quiet about any losses and want everyone to know only when they have won.

Lacks confidence and suffers from low self-esteem. Problem gamblers may well appear extremely confident on the surface which may be reflected in a flamboyant lifestyle. That outer confidence is, of course, necessary to add credence to the lies and deceptions that they practice both to get more money and to hide the real reason for it. In sharp contrast, however, their confidence in themselves is not nearly as well established. The gambling enables them to avoid facing this uncomfortable fact except at those times that heavy losses reinforce feelings of failure. Problem gamblers often mention having a strong dislike of themselves and recurrent feelings of worthlessness. Gambling helps them to avoid these feelings because they can imagine themselves as about to become rich and a huge success. These negative feelings can, in many instances, be linked to a state of depression that is commonly found among problem gamblers.

The gambler needs to be seen as an achiever. In order to overcome the negative feelings that gamblers have about themselves, they may try to create an image of being an achiever and of being special. This is necessary both as a means of boosting their own self-confidence and making sure other people recognise it – which is one reason why many gamblers when they have won will splash their money around and will buy other people presents. Those who cannot walk away with their winnings would want to make certain other customers in the casino or betting office know about their achievement. To illustrate their 'special' status they may place a greatly enlarged stake on the next race or on the following hand of cards.

Gambling is important to the gambler. Whilst it might sound a truism to say that a problem gambler loves gambling this is obviously an essential element of the profile. It is the needs that are met from the gambling which form the attraction. Gambling provides a means of escape from other pressures, it makes the gambler feel in control and empowered, and its participative nature provides a sense of achievement which is reinforced by winning. The fact that the last two of these can be sustained over long periods clearly distinguishes gambling from the pay-off that can be got from psychotropic addictions. Gambling also becomes important as a means of making money. Whilst deep down gamblers may sense that they are always going to lose they continue with a belief that because they have this special ability that they will make money from gambling. This is especially true of those who experienced a big win very early in their gambling careers. Secure in the knowledge that they *will win* again they chase a dream of reliving the thrill of that win which sustains them through a whole series of losses.

The gambler avoids responsibility. Just as gamblers wish to shelter a fragile ego from the inevitable string of losses they incur, they are at pains to avoid accepting responsibility. The fact that there is no money in the house to pay the electricity bill is not their fault – it must be because of bad financial management by their partner. Gambling and the money to sustain this habit are kept entirely separate from the rest of their lives. It is common to hear a problem gambler talk of having two piles of money: a small amount with which to meet unavoidable obligations, and a much larger pile with which to gamble. All the gambler's energy would go into ensuring there was money to gamble and would only seek to contribute to other expenditure when absolutely necessary. If confronted with this lack of financial contribution, gamblers would likely construct their response in such a way as to make the accuser feel that they were in the wrong.

The gambler is adept at lying. In order to cover their tracks and to extract more money out of whomsoever they can problem gamblers quickly learn how to become expert liars. However, the tendency to lie and create fanciful stories can begin before the onset of problem gambling. In my experience a number of such gamblers feel as if they became compulsive liars and would create a false trail even when it was not necessary. This act in itself is risk-taking behaviour which can provide a frisson of excitement in the distorted mind of a problem gambler. The construction of the lies and deceit can obviously be sustained far longer than by a person who is befuddled by the intake of a mind-altering substance, but when under pressure the problem gambler can begin to make mistakes.

Questions to Determine a Gambling Dependency

A number of questionnaires and screening devices have been designed to determine the extent to which a gambler has a problem with the activity. The following questions which have been adapted from the Gamblers Anonymous Checklist (Gamblers Anonymous 1996) provide further insight as to how gambling becomes a problem. The more replies in the affirmative, the greater the likelihood that there is a serious problem.

When you win do you have a strong desire to return and win more? This is not a particularly strong indicator as social gamblers are likely to want to 'have another go' when they have won. The difference lies in the strength of that desire and the ability to resist the urge. Problem gamblers are likely to 'chase' their wins by staying on the machine or moving to another, in an attempt to win more. A win boosts the sought-after feeling of being 'special', skilful or of having luck on their side.

After losing do you want to return as soon as possible to win back what you have lost? This is an extension of chasing losses within a single session, as not only do gamblers continue until all their money has gone but they are immediately motivated to secure more money to return and win back their losses. Quite obviously this is significant behaviour and can stand alone as an indicator of problem gambling.

Do you ever gamble longer than you planned? As the question specifies 'ever' it is something that many social gamblers may have experienced in their lifetime. When in good company and enjoying the atmosphere of the race track, casino, and so on, it is natural to want to linger longer. In this circumstance the original self-imposed limit may be reassessed without harm. However, if this overstaying and 're-planning' becomes a regular occurrence it is a useful indicator of possible problem gambling.

When not actually gambling do you spend time planning how to raise money to gamble again? This is a clear indication that gambling is beginning to dominate the person's life and is becoming a preoccupation. This is the case not only in terms of time resource and mental energy but it indicates that the person is in a gambling frame of mind even when not engaged in the activity.

Have you ever taken time out from college or work to gamble? Social gamblers may once or twice have missed the opening of a lecture or extended a lunch break because they were in the arcade or the bookies. The problem gambler is likely to be doing this on a regular basis and then lying to hide the fact.

Do you ever gamble to get away from a boring or unhappy life? When speaking to a young problem gambler the quoted trigger for gambling is often 'I was bored.' It is more likely that with time on their hands the prospect of doing something exciting that doesn't require much effort is the spur. If gambling has already invaded their life, that is likely to be the solution. This seems to be borne out by episodic problem gamblers who, when busily occupied in something of interest, do not have the urge to gamble excessively. Female gamblers who did not start gambling until they were in their late twenties or thirties often say that they started at a time when their lives were unhappy. Gambling at this time meets a need in the individual and becomes a problem when they become dependent on it.

Do you gamble to escape from worry or stress? The operative word in this question is 'escape'. As discussed in more detail elsewhere in the book, the need to escape is a powerful hook into problem gambling. While gambling, outside pressures can be forgotten for a while and, coupled with the enveloping atmosphere of many gambling environments, this can be very seductive. Answering 'yes' to this question is significant.

Does gambling cause you to suffer from sleeplessness? Problem gamblers will talk about their inability to sleep at night which probably arises from a number of factors. The adrenaline rush associated with the build-up and release of tension linked to risk taking whilst gambling would be slow to subside after gambling. The anxiety and worry associated with covering debts and raising money preys on the mind. Planning future gambling expeditions becomes a dominant thought process for the problem gambler. However, sleeplessness can be associated with a whole range of causes that have nothing to do with gambling so this question only becomes significant in association with others.

Do arguments, frustrations and disappointments make you want to gamble? The need to escape, the need to be in control, the need to feel good about yourself all feature in this particular question. Problem gamblers might also engineer arguments as a deliberate strategy, so that they can storm out of the confrontation and 'disappear' for a few hours to cool down. Answering 'yes' to this question is a reasonable indicator that gambling is seen as a comfort when things are not going well or the person is upset.

Do you ever gamble until your last pound has gone? Any gamblers who spend all the money they have on their person has almost certainly exceeded their self-imposed limit or did not set one in the first place. It is a significant sign of problem gambling when caution is thrown to the wind in the belief that the last few coins will retrieve the losses of the day. In the eventuality of a win in these circumstances problem gamblers are still unlikely to quit and will rationalise their action by the chance of winning more. In reality it prolongs the gambling experience.

Do you gamble to get money to pay debts or to solve your financial problems? The social gambler recognises that gambling is a means of buying entertainment and if you win it is an enjoyable and exciting bonus. Problem gamblers harbouring the belief that they are different and that they will win, view the act of gambling as the cure all for their financial difficulties. There are many stories of problem gamblers who, when under great pressure to repay a debt or 'borrowed' money, have managed to raise part of the sum. Instead of paying that as an instalment the amount raised is then staked on further gambling to raise the rest. Very occasionally this gamble pays off, but in most instances the money is lost and the debt mountain becomes higher still.

Are you in debt? Almost inevitably the problem gambler will be in debt. Slot machine gamblers may chase their losses but can never make up the shortfall so their debts will steadily mount up. A casino or betting office gambler may have a different pattern as, when a big win is recorded, outstanding debts may be paid off – only to reappear a short time later.

Have you ever lied to get money to gamble? If gamblers answer 'yes' to this question they have clearly reached the stage where they know that the extent of their gambling is likely to meet with disapproval. They are hiding the fact, which in itself is taking a risk.

Have you ever sold your own or your family possessions to get money to gamble or to pay gambling debts? A common occurrence for problem gamblers when the need for more money assumes paramount importance. Missing possessions can, for example, be disguised by a fake burglary or by suggesting that someone else is responsible in order to divert suspicion. If this deception is repeated it is less likely to protect the gambler. Many case histories indicate that this is the time when the extent of the gambling is discovered by the family.

Have you ever 'borrowed' without permission or stolen in order to get money? As problem gamblers have this belief of being special and that they will win with their next bet they rationalise taking money as merely borrowing for a short period before paying it back with interest. This attitude extends beyond taking from family to misappropriating other people's money for which they are responsible. Quite obviously, any gambler who is doing this has a serious problem.

Are you reluctant to spend 'gambling money' on anything else? This is an indication that gambling is taking over a person's life. Both figuratively and literally, problem gamblers will have money in two pockets; a minimum amount to cover unavoidable expenditure in one pocket and as much cash as they can accumulate in the other. As gambling money runs out they will reassess the 'unavoidable expenditure' and almost certainly take from that pocket to continue gambling. If confronted with a demand for money they would ignore 'gambling money' in their response (adding weight to the assertion that money is merely the means of carrying through the activity of gambling).

Did your gambling increase after you gave up a sport at which you were skilled? My contact with young problem gamblers over a number of years has indicated, in many cases, a definite link between sports prowess and gambling. Gambling can meet similar needs to that experienced by competitive sport: adrenaline flow, build-up and release of tension, feeling of being special, being in competition and beating the odds, feeling in control, and being the centre of attention. A further factor might be the widespread social side betting associated with sport. When winning or participating in that sport becomes more difficult the individual may turn increasingly to gambling to satisfy personal needs.

Have you lost interest in your family? There may, of course, be a number of reasons for this but problem gamblers usually have few relationships and can become alienated from the family. If they are known to be causing money problems or, because of tension, there is constant strain within the family group, gamblers will avoid facing up to the situation. Preoccupied with planning the next gambling episode or with finding more money, a problem gambler has little time or energy to consider the family.

Do you instigate rows at home in order to create an excuse to go out and gamble? Instigating an argument so as to provide an excuse to storm out is a method of securing gambling time often admitted by problem gamblers. This particular ploy serves another purpose – that of avoiding responsibility and transferring guilt to the other member of the family. Whilst this type of behaviour in itself might not be an indicator, when taken in conjunction with others it helps to confirm that gambling is the problem.

Have you ever thought seriously of suicide as a means of solving your problems? Low self-esteem, a mountain of debt, the despair when faced with a crisis from which they cannot wriggle away, and the enormity of the destruction they have wrought can engender suicidal thoughts. Committing suicide is also the ultimate power play of a 'victim'. It enables the gambler to avoid responsibility for ever, and is likely to heap lasting guilt on one or more people involved in the gambler's life.

SUMMARY

The large majority of gamblers keep their gambling under control and enjoy the experience as an exciting social activity. For a significant minority, however, it becomes what is known as 'problem gambling'.

This occurs when it begins to have serious adverse consequences on the life of the gambler or on the lives of those affected by the gambler's behaviour. Problem gambling is sometimes referred to as the hidden addiction as there are a number of factors that make it difficult to detect. These include a total commitment of resources to gambling, unrealistic expectations of the gain to be got from gambling, and the need to supplement their own disposable income with other money. Problem gamblers are often driven to using the activity of gambling as a means of feeling good about themselves. There are a number of screening devices to determine if gambling can be categorised as a problem such as those detailed in this chapter.

CHECKLIST

The following is a list of the main indicators that the gambler is becoming a problem gambler:

- Chases losses and tries to win back money lost.

- Commits an inappropriately large amount of time and finance to gambling.

- Gambling becomes an important and integral part of their lifestyle.

- Gambles frequently, for long periods and alone.

- Unwilling to repay money borrowed and is in debt.

- Commits crimes to obtain the means of gambling or to pay off pressing debts.

- Continues to gamble until all their money, including money won, is gone.

- Lies about the extent of their gambling to those closest to them.

- Is drawn to gamble as a means of escaping pressures and problems.

- The need to gamble overrides all other interests and obligations.

4   Family Factors

They fill you with the faults they had
And add some extra, just for you.

(Philip Larkin on parents, 'This Be The Verse' 1974)

There does not appear to be any real agreement as to the extent to which a propensity for heavy gambling is inherited or induced. A predisposition for risk taking can certainly be passed down the generations but it is probable that childhood learning is a primary cause of later behaviour.

Case histories of numerous problem gamblers support this assertion and commonly suggest that family factors have a significant bearing on their vulnerability towards dependency.

Studies have suggested that problem gamblers come from dysfunctional families (Lorenz 1994). However, the term 'family dysfunction' covers a multitude of situations and in itself does not convey very much. In my view every family is dysfunctional to some degree, just as there is no agreed definition of a normal family. Added to which the real effect of parents on their children can be hard to determine. Many problem gamblers need to block out all negative experiences and recall having grown up in a safe environment with supportive and loving parents. However, in a large number of cases a look at the background history can uncover attitudes and events that contributed markedly to insecurity or diminished family bonding.

Related to this is the fact that problem gamblers are very likely to have developed, from an early age, a poor opinion of themselves. Feelings of inadequacy and of being a failure are trademarks of this type of addict, especially when early experiences are reinforced later in life.

These influences are not, of course, exclusive to a gambling dependency as without a doubt the majority of the population to some degree has had similar experiences and feelings. However, they are very likely to figure significantly in a problem gambler's background and form the thread that holds together the combination of relevant predisposing factors.

CONTRIBUTARY CHILDHOOD EXPERIENCES

Individual childhood experiences are unlikely to suggest dependency but a combination make it possible that these individuals may well become problem gamblers. The following contributory experiences are drawn partly from case studies seen at the Baltimore Clinic in the US (Lorenz 1994) as well as from personal knowledge gained in working with this dependency. They have been split into those that are gambling specific and others.

Gambling Specific

Money is or has been a point of emphasis within the family. This is a factor which may help to identify a vulnerability towards gambling dependency as against a chemical addiction. The emphasis on money may be because there is, for whatever reason, an acute lack of it within the family or, in contrast, financial abundance allowed large sums to be spent on entertainment. When the acquisition of money assumes particular importance and risk taking is an acceptable method of the accumulation of wealth, gambling is only a step along the continuum.

Gambling has been an approved and accepted activity by one or both parents or by other significant adult family members. Very often problem gamblers will talk about their first experience of gambling having taken place at a young age. This might have been because they were introduced to card playing or other gambling games as a family pastime. Another common starting-point was from fathers and uncles betting on the horses or mothers and aunts playing bingo at a local social club. Studies indicate (Lorenz and Shuttleworth 1983, Lesieur and Klein 1987) that in more than an average percentage of cases there is evidence of a gambling or other dependency in the parents of problem gamblers.

In order to gain attention at an early age, the gambler learnt to emulate the role and personality of a parent who also had difficulty in controlling their gambling. Part of the family dysfunction when a parent is a problem gambler is the neglect of the children. Problem gamblers do not have time for them because, when not out at work, they are either gambling or embarked on the time-consuming business of securing money in order to continue gambling. When at home they are likely to be preoccupied with placating their partner or in studying 'form' with a mind still focused on gambling activity. The non-gambling partner, on the other hand, will be preoccupied with holding together the home and is likely to have a part- or full-time job. When the gambler is present the partner may well be focused on trying to communicate with him rather than on the children. In order to gain the attention of the gambler, a child, particularly of the same gender, realises the only way to do so is to take an interest in gambling. A mutually interesting topic of conversation can be established and children can feel a closeness to their parent when they become involved themselves in the gambling activity.

Others

Broken, disruptive or severely dysfunctional family background. As noted earlier in the chapter, this is the background experience of the majority of problem gamblers. It may be that a parent or close relative had a drink, drug or gambling dependency. Children can be traumatised when their parents separate and divorce and are further affected when a new parental role model enters the family dynamic. Violence, both physical (usually by the father) and verbal (frequently by the mother), also takes its toll.

> I started gambling from the age of seven. The reason was my nan and grandad used to be at home instead of my parents when I arrived home from school. I was frightened of my grandad and used to have nightmares about him ... I was also badly treated by my parents. I can understand this because they were badly treated by their parents – but this is really no excuse. (Alan – shop manager and recovering problem gambler, aged 28)

Death of a parent or significant other person during the early life of the gambler. The sense of loss in this situation can be overwhelming and create long-term feelings of insecurity. Coupled to this, the death of someone close can leave children questioning their own self-worth and reduce confidence levels.

> I am now 42 years old and have been gambling regularly since my mother died when I was 11. (Recovering problem gambler resident at Gordon House)

Serious injury or illness within the family or involving the gambler. When this happens to another member of the family the gambler can feel pushed out and ignored as the invalid receives all the attention. These feeling can be heightened when the illness or injury is to a sibling as the gambler can feel unworthy of attention by comparison. If it is the gambler that has experienced the illness or injury they may be the recipient of a great deal of attention. The downside, however, is that they can be left out of other family activities, may be absent from home in hospital for a prolonged period, and left feeling inadequate or less than whole.

Infidelity by one or both parents or by the gambler's partner. Infidelity by parents has a range of consequences that might adversely affect a child. The child may be party to a parent's secret affair and learn the excitement and anxiety that goes with hiding the truth. Exposure of the infidelity is almost certain to lead to strained relationships and a tense atmosphere. This form of behaviour by one or both parents can lead to the weakening of trust and to a feeling of having been let down. Separation and divorce of parents following infidelity may leave the child confused, undermined, guilty, angry and powerless to change the situation. Gambling can seem like a soothing balm in these circumstances. Similar feelings and reactions would apply to the gambler if it is their partner who has been unfaithful. Additionally this may well act as a reinforcement to adverse childhood experiences that have already made the individual vulnerable to seeking solace in gambling.

High incidence of abuse involving the gambler. Probably nothing destroys self-esteem more than suffering some form of emotional, physical or sexual abuse as a child, or of having experienced the severe trauma of being raped.

> the punishments I was given by my stepdad became more severe. The belt was hurting more, and the times I was confined to my room were getting longer. It came as a relief when, at 13, I was told that I was going to a special school. (Problem gambler, aged 25)

These humiliating and degrading acts, particularly when sustained over a long period of time, are likely to scar an individual for life. Deep-seated fears and feelings of low self-worth can be annulled temporarily by total absorption in gambling, the act of which can make the individual feel in control again. By way of illustration I recall a teenage girl who had been sexually abused as a young child by a relation. She found it difficult to communicate with any family members and could not share her feelings. She sought her own space as much as possible. After a big win on the fruit machines she used to play alone for hours, lost to the machine in her own space.

The problem gambler has in the past felt, or is currently feeling, belittled or disempowered. Expressions like low self-esteem, lacking in self-worth, having little inner confidence litter the case histories of problem gamblers. Much of this stems from gamblers having been made to feel that their own contribution was inadequate. The recollection of many problem gamblers is that of having been belittled or even scapegoated within the family, or in the school environment, even before the onset of their gambling. One powerful attraction of gambling is that it gives a feeling of empowerment and of being in control of the situation. For gamblers who feel they have little or no control over their lives and who feel put down, gambling can provide an instant restoration of being in command.

The problem gambler has faced, or is facing, difficult and stressful situations at home. There is in all of us an urge to escape from difficult and stressful predicaments and there are many ways by which this can be achieved. The total absorption of gambling, particularly in the ambience of a casino, arcade or betting office provides, for those who enjoy gambling, just such an escape route. A gambler I knew, called Mary, experienced no problem at all until, when Mary was in her thirties, her mother died. The loss of that very close relationship left her totally bereft and distraught – feelings only alleviated by spending hours in the casino. Mary's gambling quickly developed into a problem but it took her three years to recognise this fact. When she did Mary was able to address the situation and realised that whilst gambling she escaped from the extreme pain of her mother's death and was able to feel in control of her emotions.

THE PROBLEM GAMBLER'S OWN PERCEPTIONS

Early influences are highlighted when listening to personal stories told by problem gamblers. A workshop I attended at a Gamblers Anonymous convention illustrated many of these perceptions of childhood experiences. The following factors are based on the reflections of a number of problem gamblers who were courageous enough to share their thoughts as to what contributed to their dependency.

Feeling inferior to one's peer group and others. For whatever reason, inner feelings of inferiority and lack of self-worth permeate the background history of problem gamblers. In this context the inferiority refers to peer groups but its root may stem from the way the gambler has been treated within the family or how the family is perceived outside.

Using one's reputation as a gambler to cultivate status. This may be closely linked to the above. When faced with ridicule or worse by one's peers, a way out is to create an image of being different and of having a skill few others possess. Gambling provides that opportunity especially when the extent of losses can be hidden and successes made widely known. Extra status can be obtained in circumstances when the gambler acts nonchalantly to any losses sustained. Appearing philosophical about large losses can help to create a significant 'Mr Cool' image. Success in playing cards or at the arcade emphasises being special and being singled out as an achiever.

> I wanted the others at school to look up and respect me. Gambling gave me that chance and I took it. (Accountant, aged 34)

Feeling or being made to feel that one's own contribution was inadequate. Being made to feel something we have done is 'not good enough' is an experience many of us can recall. In the case of the problem gambler these experiences reoccur and the feeling of inadequacy is reinforced. Within the dynamics of the family the gambler can from an early age be ascribed a role which emphasises failure.

> My parents wanted me to do well and I began to dread the lecture I would get when they saw my end of term school reports. Average grades and those damning words 'could do better' were enough for my father to make me feel a total failure. (Businessman, aged 55)

Low self-esteem. If, as a child, you are told often enough that you are not good enough it becomes a part of your psychological make-up for the rest of your life. Problem gamblers get into a destructive spiral of reinforcing the message by their subsequent behaviour. In my view, many then derive a perverse comfort from this position, which can be extremely powerful, and excuse their actions by taking refuge in their 'badness'.

> As a child I suffered both physical and mental abuse from my father. I had a difficult childhood for many reasons which have made me what I am. (Salesman, aged 30)

The importance of winning was felt keenly from childhood. Games of chance provide an early experience of competitive play and problem gamblers will tell you how important is was for them to win. The need to be successful, an achiever, someone special, the need to move away from the bottom of the family pecking order, all contribute to the intensity.

> I was a bad loser. If it seemed likely that my brother or sisters were going to win I'd accuse them of cheating or 'accidentally' tip the board over. (Student, aged 20)

Love of gambling from an early age. The problem gamblers spoke of their early realisation that gambling felt good especially at a time when they had no obligations or responsibility. Despite regulations, with the encouragement of parents they had no difficult in gambling from a very early age.

> At the age of 7 I used to join the old men playing pitch a coin. In the end I became a lookout for these men because gambling then was illegal. My next encounter with gambling was at the age of 13 or 14. At that time my mother used to send me to the bookmakers to place her bets. I was fascinated by all the people in there, shouting and screaming at the horses they had backed. It wasn't long before I was gambling myself. (Dave – recovering problem gambler, aged 32)

Refusal to take responsibility for one's own gambling. Problem gamblers do not want to take the blame for the adverse consequences of their gambling. To do so would make them feel worse about themselves and force them to face up to the fact that gambling, which gave them so much, was causing harm. They become adept at making their parents or partner feel guilty and in transferring the responsibility to them.

> Mum found out I was gambling when the police brought me home for stealing a bike. When she asked why I said it was her fault for making me unhappy – she and Dad had split up and she'd taken me away from Blackburn where my friends were. (Simon – trainee chef, aged 23)

The gambler perceives a lack or loss of affection by one or both parents. When you talk with the parents of a problem gambler their perception is that of having offered consistent love. The gambler's perception is often very different, seeing that love as highly conditional or lacking in some regard. The experience of Gordon House (see Chapter 11) is that many residents recall that their parent(s) demonstrated a lack of love by, for instance, sending them away to boarding school when they did not want to go. In many instances this lack of love and affection was very real as one or both parents were either absent from infancy or were not there during the gambler's formative years.

> I come from a single-parent family. I still remember at the age of 8 the rejection of chasing my mum down the road crying 'Where are you going?' There was no reply. She just walked away and left us. (Kevin – recovering problem gambler)

EARLY EXPERIENCES REINFORCED

The majority of problem gamblers first get involved in the activity in their early teens. By the time problem gamblers set up home with a partner and/or get married, their pattern of gambling is well established. It is quite likely that they will let their partner know they gamble, but be very careful to hide the extent to which they bet on the horses, frequent the casino, and so on. One of their attractive qualities may centre around the excitement their partner shares at, for instance, a day at the races. Gifts from winnings, or even from money obtained elsewhere, may help convince the partner that life is great. Add to this the outwardly attractive charm and personality gamblers can exude and it is easy to see why they might appear a good prospect. I have been told by their partners on numerous occasions that when not gambling their other half is a person with many excellent qualities and that, despite everything, they still love them.

From the gamblers' point of view a good relationship appears to provide the acceptance and affection they lacked in childhood. Undoubtedly, for some, the need to gamble diminishes when a deeply satisfying relationship is found, but for others the needs met from gambling hold them in the dependency. Embellishing stories, hiding painful episodes and creating a false picture are well-established ploys that the gambler may have been using for years. It is also probable that when they first meet their life partner they fabricate some story which they then need to perpetuate – the trail of deceit has already begun.

> I told Mandy I was a dealer on the stock market and got bonuses for the long hours I put in ... long hours at the bookies more like. (Fred – shop manager and former gambler)

As the pattern of problem gambling continues so the edifice of deceit grows. The gambler will become more withdrawn, more unreliable and frequently absent. Suspicions harboured by the partner will add to the tension and if articulated are likely to provoke adamant denial. The gambler will quite likely have a job that allows unaccountable time – travelling salesman for instance – as this provides a ready-made cover for absences. If the gambler's circumstances do not provide natural opportunities for long periods away from home they will invent them.

> My parents thought I had this smashing job as a night club manager. Truth was my work was stealing to get enough to stay in the casino all night. (Paul – unemployed, a recovering problem gambler, aged 40)

It always seems remarkable to me that so many women allow the man in a partnership to control the financial affairs. In the case of a problem gambler they would see it as essential that they controlled the money. Glib lies, half-truths and the wherewithal to maintain a good lifestyle all help allay suspicion and mute any concern. As the debts mount the gambler goes to great lengths to hide the extent of the financial mess but will only pay out when it is absolutely essential. In my experience it is common for gamblers to waylay the postman to remove all bills and financial demands. The first time a significant debt situation is exposed, gamblers will have their excuses ready and, unless the partner has other reasons to be unhappy, are likely to be given the benefit of the doubt. It is at this stage that the partner is, or other family members are, called upon to bail them out – reassured by promises from the gambler that the situation will not occur again. It may be at this stage that the partner begins to realise the extent of the gambling, but I have heard many stories where they are still totally ignorant of the real cause of the debt. Doubts may form in their mind, however, and if a member of the extended family has been critical of the relationship the partner may begin to feel vulnerable.

> When we married I said I would take care of all the bills and Ann happily agreed. She even asked me to look after the bank accounts as she got into a muddle with money! (Trevor – accountant and former gambler)

It is also quite likely that the gambler will blame the partner for the debts or, when known, the extent of the gambling. There are endless ways of making the other person feel guilty and responsible and, as the gambler is skilled at using words to good effect, successfully transfers blame. 'If you hadn't insisted we take that expensive holiday last year', 'If you got yourself a proper job', 'I work all the hours I can to bring money in for you and the kids', 'Can't I spend some of the money I earn on something I enjoy?'

However, gamblers wish to avoid being confronted with the extent of the gambling as that brings the possibility of exposure. They will do their best to avoid an explanation by denial and by lying. The denial begins, of course within the gamblers' own minds as they do not want to believe that their gambling is out of control and that they are going to carry on losing. If a clash seems inevitable gamblers may deliberately turn the conversation into an angry argument. This might have two pay-offs for the gambler. First, it allows them to manipulate the argument away from a focus on the gambling and onto aspects of the partner's failings. Second, it provides an escape route – they can storm out of the house and stay away for hours. This is likely to leave the partner distressed, feeling guilty, and frustrated that nothing has been resolved. This in turn usually leads both people to become further withdrawn from one another, leaves them with unsatisfied needs and weakens the essential basis for a positive relationship.

As soon as I got in the door she'd ask what had I done today. The interest was genuine but I threw it in her face, accused her of checking up on me, got into a rage and stormed off to a night at the dogs. (Serving prisoner and recovering problem gambler, aged 38)

SUMMARY

There are a number of family factors and experiences that can contribute towards a gambler being particularly vulnerable to becoming dependent on the activity. Many of them are subsequently reinforced later in their lives. Some of them are specific to gambling, such as money being a major point of emphasis within the home, while others could equally relate to individuals in difficulty with another addictive behaviour, such as being abused as a child. A problem gambler's own perceptions include feelings of inferiority, of not being valued and of finding gambling attractive from an early age.

CHECKLIST

The following list indicates some of the major family factors and experiences that might contribute towards the development of problem gambling:

Gambling Specific

- Money has been a point of emphasis in the family.

- Gambling was an approved family activity.

- Early realisation that gambling was a means of achieving status.

- Need to win and to feel 'special' important.

- Passes responsibility for consequences of gambling to parents or partner.

General Factors

- Significantly dysfunctional family upbringing.

- Death of a parent or significant other family member.

- Serious injury or illness to the gambler or significant other family member.

- Childhood experience of emotional, physical or sexual abuse.

- Was belittled as a child and made to feel own contribution was inadequate.

- Feelings of low self-esteem.

- Felt inferior to peer group and to others.

- Perceived lack of love and affection by one or both parents.

5   Young People and
Problem Gambling

They eat your money and you can get carried away with them.

(Female fruit machine player, aged 12)

Gambling is attractive to young people for a number of reasons. The natural human trait of risk taking is magnified during our teenage years as we become aware of our personal power and ability for self-expression. Experimentation and testing boundaries are a healthy aspect of the transition from child to adult. Gambling, portrayed as an adult activity, is one such area for exploration. The prospect of emulating adults whilst free of their controlling influence by playing in the arcade, buying scratchcards or gambling in a card game has great appeal. The buzz from this is likely to be enhanced when it takes place in a safe social environment with a group of peers.

In many instances a young person is first introduced to gambling or encouraged to try it by a parent or other family member, sometimes at a very early age.

> John was 10 when he started to play on fruit machines whilst on holiday at a seaside caravan site. He was given a daily allowance by his parents to spend in the arcade. (Case history extract of teenager from the north of England)

Recently the encouragement to gamble has been endorsed by the media and, indeed, by the government. The introduction of the National Lottery has proved a catalyst in changing perceptions about gambling. Young people are no longer faced with the double message of 'Well yes, gambling is allowed but it is not really something you *should* be doing.' The media promotion, particularly television, of the Lottery and a former assertion that 'it is just a harmless flutter' have done much to create the perception that gambling is good for you. It remains to be seen as to how this message about gambling, especially when reinforced with the prospect – however remote – of a prize substantial enough to change your lifestyle, will impinge upon vulnerable young people. It seems quite possible that those with a desperate need to 'chase the dream' may neglect their education or avoid working as they cling to a belief that they are special and *will* win the National Lottery jackpot. This is brought out in a recent exploratory investigation of the psychosocial effects on eleven- to fifteen-year-olds gambling on the National Lottery and scratchcards:

> A significant number of the participants thought that they would win a lot of money on either the National Lottery (21%) or scratchcards (25%) [a lot of money was defined as over one million pounds by 67 per cent of the participants]. (Wood and Griffiths 1998, p. 7)

However, the Lottery only opens the door as the interest it stimulates encourages experimentation in other gambling activities. In recent times the preferred gambling mode for young people has, without doubt, been that of the fruit machine. The environment of the arcade enhances the attraction: the noise, flashing lights, absence of parental supervision, a 'cool' meeting place, somewhere to show off skills and, for many gamblers, a means of gaining kudos.

> The graphics, the excitement, and the challenge, the technology is great, I feel like I'm in space. (Male gambler from South Wales, aged 14)

For the majority of these young gamblers, like their older counterparts, they treat gambling as an occasional fun social activity. However, as research has shown (Fisher 1993, Griffiths 1995) between 3 per cent and 7 per cent of the three million adolescents who play fruit machines are problem gamblers. For this small but significant number of teenagers the need to continue playing becomes irresistible and, for many of them, very destructive.

Getting Involved

That first taste of gambling may have come from a family game or seeing parents gamble on the Grand National or the Lottery. The playground provides an environment where that first vicarious experience can be turned into participation. An innocent game of marbles takes on a different connotation when sweets or pocket money is staked. Many gamblers record their first experience of gambling as playing 'pitch and toss' – a simple form of gambling where coins are tossed against a wall. The winner, who collects all the coins in the game, is the person whose coin lands closest to the wall. Before the 1990s the next stage in getting involved was, despite age restrictions, very often a bet on the horses.

> I had my first bet at 13 years of age when my mother put a bet on the Grand National for me. Like most gamblers my first wager won. (Steve – hotel manager, aged 40)

In more recent times playing the fruit machines or, perhaps because of the added 'dare' factor, buying scratchcards whilst under the legal minimum age has become the first real taste of gambling. By the time a child is in his or her early teens there is a 75 per cent chance that he or she has started gambling (Fisher 1998).

When you speak with young people about fruit machine playing they perceive a number of factors that first attracted them to this form of gambling. The following have been drawn from my own conversations with young gamblers, as well as from a number of sources and particularly the work of Dr Mark Griffiths.

Initial attraction. There are a number of reasons cited by young gamblers for being first attracted to gambling. These include the chance to win money, to have fun, for the challenge, because their parents or their friends played, or because the chance to explore adult pastimes was limited. In the case of slot machines two more can be added: the desire to beat the machine and the atmosphere of the amusement arcade.

Sociological factors. Parental gambling could play a part in putting a seal of approval on the activity but it is more likely that a parent or family member had introduced the child to playing on the machine. In many instances this was reinforced on holiday when the young player would be given money to spent in the arcade. For many the first encounter with a fruit machine was in a local cafe or fish and chip shop. Access to these machines is usually less restricted than to those in an arcade and very young children can be drawn by the noise and the lights. Peer group pressure does not seem to apply to initial play although it is a natural tendency to want to join in an activity with your friends.

To win money. The reason for playing machines often cited by young teenagers is to win money.

> You can win more money than you put in. (Schoolgirl, aged 12)

At this age the child has learnt the power of money but not the responsibility that goes with it. Children do not understand the economics of gambling and care little for random selection and payout ratios. Many of them, therefore, see gambling on machines as easy money and only learn by painful experience that this is not the case. However, when you do not have a source of income or only a meagre one, the possibility of a machine presenting you with cash can take on fanciful proportions. This is one reason why the easy accessibility of fruit machines to children in their early teens carries a very real danger.

To show off their skill. In this regard playing the fruit machine is viewed as an extension of a video game machine. Regular players and those with an immediate aptitude for machine play can make an initial stake last a little longer. Whilst it is true to say that familiarity with the machines' playing characteristics combined with good hand and eye co-ordination are likely to maximise the opportunity for extended play, control is really an illusion. Some of the skills players say they possess have been described as 'idiot skill' (Griffiths 1995), such as using feature buttons to hold winning symbols or not continuing to play a machine that has just paid out the jackpot. The exception to this is in regard to those few players who possess the ability to learn the reels and are very disciplined in their play (Fisher 1993). Young men with the need to feel a sense of kudos, to be competitive and who gravitate towards the world of machines, are most likely to be attracted to fruit machines because of the apparent skill factor. Playing on the machines can make them feel empowered and in control of the game.

To combat negative feelings. A common response as to why a young person will play on the machines is, 'because when I am bored it gives me something to do'. As long as you have the money the fruit machine can provide an instant activity that doesn't require physical exertion (apart from getting there) or mental ability. Added to which feelings of being downhearted or depressed can be banished whilst absorbed in the interaction with a fruit machine. Similarly, pressures and problems elsewhere in their lives can be forgotten whilst indulging in the fantasy world of the intense gambler. The machine provides an escape route into a private space occupied only by the player and the machine.

For the 'buzz'. As mentioned in Chapter 2, the buzz associated with gambling is a powerful attraction. For young fruit machine players this is a particularly important element. The excitement generated by the flashing lights, the sound of coins dropping into a tin tray, the music blaring away in the arcade, and the very feel of the surroundings all combine to build up the excitement. Because the machine affords the chance for rapid play that can be repeated every few seconds the build-up and release of tension create a frisson of excitement that is increased when you win or nearly win.

These powerful feelings provide, for many young teenagers, the sort of thrill that appeals to their adolescent view of life – an opportunity to experience and create risk.

Crossing the Line

When the need for the prop provided by gambling on a slot machine increases in importance it is very easy for a young person to cross the line from social to problem gambling. Expanding on some of the reasons for involvement discussed earlier in this chapter they provide useful indications as to how and why gambling on machines can turn into a serious dependency. The following hooks that lead to problem gambling by young people are drawn mainly from the author's experience of working with this group and from *The Young Fruit Machine Player* (Bellringer and Fisher, 1997).

To escape. It is both the game and the venue that provide a strong attraction for the young player whose motivation for playing is primarily to escape. The machine is a source of non-human interaction that has been described as an 'electronic friend' (Griffiths 1991). In talking with young problem gamblers it became clear to me that this interaction with the machine is seen by them as safer than human relationships. The affinity with the machine becomes totally absorbing and all other problems can be blocked out. This occurs even in the face of an obvious paradox in that it is likely that losing the money obtained to gamble is inevitably going to compound any worry. As long as the action of gambling lasts, however, this anxiety can be minimised or temporarily forgotten. Whilst playing, the gambler can feel in control and safe from the outside world, cocooned in a fantasy that is enhanced by the ambience of the amusement arcade. The added attraction of the gambling venue should not be underestimated as for many pushing open the glass doors of the arcade is like Alice stepping through the looking-glass. Once inside the warm embrace of the gambling arena gamblers may feel comfortable being surrounded by others or may wish to create a lonely space for themselves. Either way they can be among others without any need to risk intimate social contact. The problem gambler needing to escape is, therefore, likely to be socially isolated and is quite likely to feel depressed. Playing on the machines becomes the centre of his or her life, and nothing else matters.

> I ate, slept and breathed gambling machines ... I couldn't even find time to spend with the people I loved. ... The machines were more important than anything or anyone else. (Written response by an eleven-year-old to a postal study (Griffiths 1995))

It is important to point out that for young persons drawn to a machine because of a need to escape, the primary problem does not lie with the act of gambling. It is the need to escape which has to be addressed if they are successfully to break free of the dependency. (The implications of this in tackling problem gambling are looked at in more detail in Chapter 9.)

For empowerment. Whilst it may seem paradoxical, particularly when you are losing, gambling can provide a strong sense of being in control and of feeling powerful. The very fact that they have the means to partake in the game gives problem gamblers a feeling of being in charge. As they face the machine, the challenge of beating the system, of winning against the odds, adds to the anticipation. As long as they have the money to continue this challenge the sensation of being in control of the situation persists. When they win this feeling is reinforced and it does much to counterbalance the perception of feeling disempowered elsewhere in their lives.

Linked to that need to feel in control is a keen interest in the technicality of playing the game. For these gamblers the problem-solving opportunity provided by the gambling activity is very appealing, and a necessary adjunct to the sense of being in charge. The machine provides a challenge to the technical skill of the player that involves a decision-making process around knowledge of the reels and the use of the feature buttons. The fact that in reality the buttons only provide an illusion of control does not impinge on this type of machine player. The need to continue playing so as to prolong the feeling of empowerment overrides any thought about quitting. This applies regardless of whether they have won or whether they are persistently losing. This type of problem gambler will, therefore, not be able to exercise any discipline over their play and will stay on the machine until all their money has been spent. Prolonging the activity as long as possible rather than winning money is again the object of the exercise, and loss-chasing behaviour is inevitable. So the problem gambler primarily motivated to gamble for empowerment is likely to spend hours gambling and the rest of the time gathering sufficient money to get back to the machine and the intimacy of the technical challenge.

When they are forced to walk away because their money has been spent the feelings of failure and of having lost out in terms of control become magnified. This resultant low reinforces any depressive symptoms and acts as a spur to renewing the search for money. Taking the earliest opportunity to re-engage with the technical challenge and experience that sense of purpose and power becomes the imperative.

The buzz. An essential contribution to the attraction of gambling is that of excitement – the thrill that can be obtained both from anticipation and participation. The build-up and release of tension coupled to the risk of losing the stake provides a powerful motivator for many gamblers. In the case of a three-reel slot machine the reels only spin for a total of five seconds (unless they are delayed by use of certain feature buttons). That means that even by doubling that time-span to include putting in more money, paying out and so on, it is easily possible to have six goes per minute. In theory twelve goes per minute can be achieved which, for a 25p stake, has a cost factor of £3 per minute. Each time the stake is committed it can provide a tremor of anticipation which becomes a definite buzz when the machine records a win. In fact a definite buzz will also be felt if you perceive that you have nearly won – a feature built into the design of machines (Griffiths 1995).

For the problem gambler hooked on the buzz, the feelings associated with being 'in the action', with the competition against the machine or with being a success, becomes an overwhelming driving force. Gambling itself, as a form of risk-taking behaviour, is the primary motivation to stay at the machine. Like the gambler motivated by the need to feel empowered, the craving to be in on the action enslaves the player to the machine for as long as possible. In my experience the buzz obtained from gambling for some is extended to that need to get gambling money. For this type of young problem gambler the risks associated with conning friends and neighbours out of cash or in stealing money, in itself provides a thrill. This behaviour can replicate the experience of excited anticipation, build-up of tension and release. Actually obtaining money means a greater buzz.

As mentioned in Chapter 3, I have noticed over a number of years that a large percentage of young problem gamblers who are primarily motivated by the buzz are also adept at a particular sport. They have experienced the anticipation, tension, relief and euphoria associated with competitive sport. Their prowess has taken them to a level of success, recognition and self-satisfaction – but they need more. Because of injury, better quality opposition or just a need to go higher the young person turns to gambling to sustain the good feelings. From the many cases I have dealt with the action of competitive sport and the action of gambling, particularly slot machines, appear to meet similar needs.

In contrast to being hooked by the need to escape or to feel empowered, the primary problem for the gambler motivated by the buzz is the need to take risks.

> I would always look forward tremendously to playing machines and couldn't get to them fast enough. I always got this kind of feeling of being 'high' or 'stoned'.... . Since becoming hooked I've never been able to stop playing a machine once I've started. (Young county class swimmer (Griffiths 1995, p. 184))

CASE HISTORY

Some of these aspects of getting involved are brought out in the following case history that was written by Fred, a university student:

> When most people walk into a pub or the Student Union bar they will buy a drink, spot a few friends and have a bit of a laugh – a year ago it was impossible for me, like all compulsive gamblers, to do that.

> The moment I walked into the Union bar the machines in the corner, which are just part of the decor, seemed to tower above me. I feel my level of excitement heighten and thoughts race through my mind as to whether I'd win if I put money in them. The feeling becomes so overwhelming that any thoughts of 'I might lose' are lost in the classic 'OK, but only a couple of quid' which seems to sweep in. Before I know it I'm standing directly in front of the machine with coins in my hand.

> The first coin drops in the machine and sparks off a simultaneous feeling of both warmth and yet dismay. You know that you have just started a chain reaction, you have got a lot of money on you and your cash card is in your pocket. I won't explain the course of events that happens in this type of incident

because if you are a compulsive gambler ... you'll know. The most annoying thing that people with no problem must realise is that gamblers are not 'half way' to being cured when they realise they have a problem. Every fruit machine fanatic will tell you that they can see other people do the same as them. You can see yourself do it time and time again yet still persist. Maybe it is because after losing so much money and deceiving people so close to you it is done out of frustration in the seemingly eternal quest to make some money and start afresh.

However, as long as the priorities are in this order you can never sort the problem out and lead a normal life. The problem simply snowballs into a 'no win' predicament. The money is lost and you can't win it back. GamCare made me see things differently and I strongly believe if I had not gone to see them, in a year's time I would either be dead or in jail.

I think my addiction stems from when I was about twelve years old. My parents took me and a friend every Easter to the south coast every week. Ryan and I used to play on 2p machines and waterfall machines (pushers). The amounts we spent grew and by the age of sixteen the £200 jackpot machines in our local snooker hall became our goal. A slow and gradual progression evolved of spending more and more money. I believed I could beat the machine with more practice, which justified the disappearance of money to myself. The problem changed my entire personality from extrovert to a very enclosed introverted and deceptive person.

When the problem reached its peak I was at my first year at university. I could not afford to pay my rent as I had spent my student loan and had a £600 overdraft. I was at rock bottom. My mum sent me over £200 for my car tax and I remember spending it all on the fruit machines at the Union bar. The moment the last reel spun I felt sick inside, almost suicidal. When you are a machine addict you can't blame anyone but yourself. My mum couldn't afford to give me the tax money herself, but she did and yet I just watched her struggle on. I had just put nails in my own coffin. As I got back to the halls there was a parcel from my mum. I opened it and found a letter inside saying the family loved me very much. I broke down. All the anger inside me finally exploded. I could not hide behind the lies and deception any more. I packed my bags the next day and went home.

A Conspiracy of Factors

The hooks into young problem gambling do not provide the only motivation to cross the line and should never be taken in isolation. It is certain that gamblers will have been driven to seek their needs being met from this activity by a combination of factors. The gambler driven by the buzz may also have a strong need to feel empowered, as would the person who desires to escape from pressures and problems.

The value of identifying the relevant hooks when working with young problem gamblers is that of exploring reasons that lie behind the gambling and in developing strategies to break free of the dependency (see Chapter 9).

Other factors will also play their part in pushing a young person over the line that divides the social from the problem gambler. Self-esteem is important to all of us and, for one reason or another, it can be a fragile commodity even in the most successful members of society. Almost without exception problem gamblers struggle with their self-esteem; it is all too easily damaged or broken down. Gambling provides a mental crutch that shores up their esteem. It allows the gambler to feel good, secure and able to stand up and be counted. Others can see the gambler as a participating somebody. The drawback with a mental crutch is that unless you make the effort to discard it you can become dependent on it. Physical crutches have obvious limitations and are visible reminders of not being whole which in turn adds to the incentive to move on. The crutch provided by gambling is unseen by others but enables the afflicted person to believe they have got their act together. It can make them feel like a 'somebody'. The motivation to discard this support is much less tangible and only arises when losses and the consequences of gambling appear overwhelming. The fear of throwing away this psychological support and all that goes with it assumes mammoth proportions – it is easier to lean on the crutch.

The lack of self-esteem, however caused, is created in childhood and erupts during adolescence. This time of transition is, even to a relatively stable teenager, a roller-coaster of emotional, spiritual and physical change. Those young people who are struggling with feelings of self-worth may find themselves particularly vulnerable to the seductive attraction of gambling. Not only does it provide an activity that is seen to be adult, once involved it meets some of those inner needs and makes the players feel good about themselves.

As was suggested in Chapter 4 the fragility of self-esteem may well have arisen from early experiences of being belittled, of being compared unfavourably with peers, or of being emotionally, physically or sexually abused. Whilst it is difficult to draw hard conclusions, when these influences combine, it is my opinion that they can create a vulnerability towards a gambling dependency. The need to be special, to prove one's value, to win and to appear successful become forceful motivators.

The arena of the amusement arcade is an important factor in providing the conditions to experience and to get hooked into slot machine playing. Without doubt it is a young person's space, relatively free of parental control, a good meeting-point, and a noisy, boldly lit environment attractive to that age group. Whilst the very first experience of playing a machine may have taken place years earlier it is the amusement arcade that, for many young teenagers, is *the* place to gather. Add to that the need, between young men, to compete and to demonstrate their skills in this electronic gladiatorial zone, playing the machines can become a rite of passage. For those who have been unable to impress their peers in any other dimension, this provides an opportunity for status enhancement as 'a gambler'. Kudos can be achieved either by being successful at playing the machines or by appearing nonchalantly cool when losing. Those who become reliant on the activity of gambling to maintain peer group status feel compelled to sustain the image that they have created. By the time they have crossed the line into problem gambling and have lost face because of borrowing money or by excluding themselves from other peer activities, it is too late to break free.

SUMMARY

Gambling is a very attractive activity for the majority of young people and they become involved for a variety of reasons. Like adults, most young gamblers keep their participation to an occasional social pastime, but for a small yet significant minority it becomes a serious problem that begins to dominate their lives. There are a number of factors that contribute to the onset of young problem gambling. Three that can be identified as significant hooks are the need to escape, the need to feel in control and the desire for the buzz. However, these should never be considered in isolation to one another or, for that matter, without taking into consideration other factors that are relevant to the individual young person.

CHECKLIST

The following lists some of the elements of the three significant hooks into young problem gambling and is an expansion of that compiled from *The Young Fruit Machine Player* (Bellringer and Fisher 1997).

Escape

- Motivated by the need to escape from overwhelming problems.
- Usually depressed and may be socially isolated.
- Feels powerless and lacks control.
- Playing machines gives them back a feeling of power.
- Both the machines and the venue contribute to the ability to escape.
- The arcade provides an opportunity for non-intimate social contact.
- The machines are a source of non-human interaction.
- A machine can become an 'electronic friend'.
- Problems are forgotten as machine interaction is totally absorbing.
- Gambling is almost certainly a secondary problem.

Empowerment

- Likely to play alone and to resent the presence of others.
- Fascinated with the working of the machine.
- Motivated by feeling empowered and in command of the situation.
- Also motivated by the interaction with the machine.
- Can become preoccupied with game techniques.
- Will play until money runs out.
- Cannot sustain self-discipline.
- Chases losses.
- Determined to beat the machine.

- Often remorseful and self-deprecating.
- Lacks patience and finds it difficult to control emotions.
- Likely to become obsessed with playing machines.

The 'Buzz'

- Motivated by the anticipation, tension, excitement and thrill of the game.
- Gets a buzz from the flow of adrenaline.
- Attracted to the rapid cycle of wagering, anticipation and release.
- Excitement enhanced by feeling like an adult when gambling.
- Similar needs met to those experienced by successful competitive sports activity.
- Arcade environment creates an atmosphere that adds to the excitement.
- Risk taking is an important element in the attraction.
- The risk taking can be extended to obtaining further gambling money.

6   The Effect of a Gambling Dependency

*My addiction has ruined my life, I have lived in squalor
and had my relationships destroyed by it.*

(South coast chef, aged 25)

Gambling is primarily a psychological dependency. The mental prop it provides is sufficiently strong to deflect otherwise rational people into a lifestyle that revolves around the need to gamble. Severe problem gamblers will spend their whole waking lives either gambling, planning the next session or obtaining the means to carry on the activity. As with other addictions, the problem gambler becomes driven by the need for 'a fix' which, as tolerance grows, requires a larger pay-off to reach a satisfactory level of relief.

In my view, a gambling dependency is as harmful as any other addiction with the exception of the physical damage that is caused by ingesting chemical substances. It can be responsible for severely negative affects such as:

- the consumption of vast amounts of time and money
- the disintegration of relationships
- the pain and suffering felt by the gambler and others
- physical ailments and impaired health
  (for example, nausea, stomach upsets, insomnia)
- crime
  (for example, embezzlement, theft, fraud)
- humiliation and degradation
- further depression and despair
- suicide

Definitions of Problem Gambling

Problem, pathological, compulsive, addictive, excessive are just some of the words used to describe gambling when it is out of control and having an adverse effect on the gambler's life. The most commonly used and generally accepted description is that of 'problem gambling'. There are a number of definitions used to describe the phenomenon of problem gambling but they all tend to contain the following elements. This theoretical description has been supported by my own experience in working over a number of years with problem gamblers.

They are unable to stop whether winning or losing. Although problem gamblers may say that they are gambling to win, money is purely the vehicle that allows them to continue the activity. It ceases to have monetary value except perhaps that demonstrating having won a large amount provides a boost to their ego. Staying in the activity is the real goal, so winnings will go back into the machine, or allow the gambler to up the stakes in the next race or spin of the wheel.

The need to gamble overrides all other considerations. A problem gambler desperate for money is likely to resort to anything to obtain it. In recent times there have been reported cases of murder, the collapse of well-established businesses, and of apparently successful lives thrown away. In listening to the painful personal stories of problem gamblers, for most there is a progressive slide into a world dominated by the need to gamble. Lying, cheating and stealing from the family, the employer and the wider community become commonplace activities. Gamblers construct a web of deceit that embraces every waking moment of their lives.

A psychological dependency is formed to the mood modification experienced when gambling. The good feelings obtained whilst gambling form an obsessive need that drives the problem gambler to repeat the experience for as long and as frequently as possible. Whether their motivation to gamble is primarily to get the buzz, to feel empowered or to escape, they are compelled to get at the action time and time again.

The Stages of a Gambling Dependency

It is said that there are three distinct phases to forming a dependency on gambling.

The winning phase often occurs the very first time the individual gambles seriously. An early significant win helps boost the ego, leading the gambler to believe that they are lucky by nature, skilled at this activity, special, and an achiever. During the career of the problem gambler this winning phase may return, which only serves further to justify their continuing with the activity – the long-awaited turn in fortune has arrived. However, this winning phase may be very short-lived, may begin to occur spasmodically, or may reappear briefly to tantalise the gambler.

The losing phase may creep up on the problem gambler slowly, so lulling them into a false sense of security. Added to which, problem gamblers very soon dismiss their losses, seeing them as only a temporary setback that precedes ultimate and total success. However, the losing phase tends to be prolonged and eats away at the gambler's own resources before precipitating the need to obtain money from elsewhere. Gamblers sustain themselves during this stage of their gambling with the memory of that first significant win bolstered by a belief that renewed success is only a bet away.

The desperation stage develops as the losing continues, the debts begin to mount and/or relationship stresses become acute. I have found in listening to problem gamblers that the trigger into desperation very often occurs when they cannot cover a debt that is being called in. It may be money that has been 'borrowed' from their employer, it may be pressure from a loan shark, or it may be the imminent risk of discovery that they have misappropriated cash. This crisis precipitates crossing the line into illegal or immoral behaviour. This line may also be crossed by those who had hitherto avoided large debts by using up their own resources. As they are driven to up the stakes in order to sustain their 'high', the demand for money outstrips the available resources and they resort to acts of desperation.

Even when a gambler has reached this desperation stage the activity may continue unabated for several years. Denial of being in this state is commonplace as the need to cling to a shred of self-belief overrides any rational thinking as to quitting. In my experience, many problem gamblers, even when faced with traumatic events such as criminal conviction, separation from their family, or the collapse of their own business enterprise, only pay lip service to addressing the problem. Inwardly they still believe it will all change and everything that has happened to them is because of some external event in their life or because of the failings of others.

Many who have gone to prison seem to adapt readily to that environment which actually helps them to avoid personal responsibility and enables them to carry on their gambling. It is a time when I have heard many promises made which evaporate as soon as the gambler walks out through the prison gates.

In addition to the three phases of gambling dependency, there is the possibility of a fourth and final phase that has been termed **rock bottom** by the fellowship of Gamblers Anonymous. It is one that some problem gamblers never reach. They stay in denial all their lives until death or infirmity curtail the destructive path through life. For others, facing rock bottom is circumvented by a successful suicide attempt – a last act of avoidance of responsibility for the mess of their own and others' lives. An unsuccessful attempt on their life does, however, become the rock bottom for many a problem gambler. The repercussions make further denial untenable or perhaps the care shown to them provides a bridge back from the chasm.

For others it is the exposure of all the deceit, the mountain of debts, the fabrication of a non-existent lifestyle. The point of deep crisis makes avoidance of reflection more difficult. This is especially the case when the gambler is faced with the immediate prospect of a sharp deterioration in their environment and status. The removal of and isolation from close family members, the real prospect of prosecution, the possibility of a severe prison sentence, or an overwhelming sense of shame and humiliation, may all play their part in motivating the gambler to change.

The Effect on the Gambler

It is arguable as to who is most affected by a gambling dependency. Problem gamblers themselves are deeply affected as they experience a roller-coaster of a ride that has more troughs than peaks and which eventually plunges down out of control.

Creating a deception. The need to hide the fact that more resources are going into gambling than they want known comes first. This may start at a low level but becomes more serious when they begin to lie in order to deny their gambling. The denial can simply be a blunt refutation of a question or, as a means of avoiding confrontation, a double image is created whereby the gamblers appear to be successful in a way that meets approval:

> I continued to gamble on fruit machines all through my school days. My way of hiding it from my family and friends was to be brilliant in school. I figured that if I were an excellent student it would be a good cover for my gambling. At the time my parents ran a small shop and I would help out on Saturdays. It became my day to steal money for the week's gambling. I would usually take between £50 and £75 every weekend. (Gordon House resident)

The lies become a web of deceit as the need to get money becomes more urgent when, for example, the stage of conning people out of money is reached or, indeed, to cover up criminal activity.

A cheating job. Problem gamblers have a remarkable habit of getting themselves into a job that allows them unaccountable time and/or entails handling money. It may be because many of them have a head for figures, or possibly because they have leant how to talk their way into employment regardless of either lack of qualifications or a poor work record. Having created the ideal opening for themselves they cannot resist the temptation to exploit the situation – and set in train a destructive domino effect.

> When I left the Army I went home to Northern Ireland and joined the civil service. They gave me a laughable job for a compulsive gambler – wages clerk dealing with thousands of pounds every week! Whilst with the civil service I married and had a son, but ended up losing my job, my house, my wife and my son after being sent to jail for stealing thousands of pounds from my employer so that I could carry on with my gambling. (Business administrator, aged 42)

An interesting observation I have made is that when problem gamblers are able to break their dependency they often make a success of their working life ... using their knowledge of figures and tendency to calculate risks to constructive advantage.

A destructive substitute. Earlier in the book I mentioned the lack of parental affection being a significant contributory factor to a gambling dependency. Poor childhood experiences leave a yearning for something to fill the void. Gambling, as we have discussed, appears to meet the basic human needs of being wanted and of making oneself feel good. When that need manifests itself at a very young age, gamblingis usually more readily available – via fruit machines – than alcohol or drugs. Once established the dependency becomes hard to shift as fear of losing the 'relationship' binds the young person tightly to the activity.

> I started pinching milk money, robbing the school, conning people out of money before I reached the age of ten. Running away from home was rather frequent. At the end of the day all I wanted was to be loved and paid some attention. (Recovering problem gambler, aged 37)

The damage is compounded by the need to spend more and more of one's resources involved in gambling. Through the unavailability of time and the borrowing that is not repaid the gambler becomes further isolated from real relationships and relies more on the gambling activity.

Into a trance. Many problem gamblers I have spoken with talk of going into a trance-like state and that their day becomes totally orientated on the activity of gambling, on raising more money to gamble with, or on planning the next episode. Every waking moment becomes, for some, occupied by gambling and every day-to-day situation is manipulated to fit into this mind-set.

> The trouble started when I was about 19. By this stage I was gambling nearly every day and losing a lot of money. This caused the start of what I call my zombie period. I used to go to work in the mornings, slip out to the bookies in my lunch and break periods to place bets and watch the horse and dog racing. My working week went like that every day. I started excluding myself from my friends and my family. I stopped going out at night and over time I lost all my 'get up and go'. I became lonely and depressed; I lost all my confidence and self-worth. My life was hell. (Trainee engineer, aged 25)

It is possible that this is a time when the gamblers' own defence mechanism of denial begins to crack. They appear to be acting on 'automatic-pilot' which, after a prolonged period becomes totally exhausting and debilitating.

Causing heartache. The gambling can cause both internal and external conflict. If the gambler has managed to construct the appearance of a settled and successful life they will begin to feel the dichotomy between the feelings from this lifestyle and those to be got from gambling. I have heard many gamblers who have settled into a relationship with a partner say that for a time, maybe lasting years, they reduced or stopped their gambling. For a number of problem gamblers the ingredients in that relationship are strong enough to break the dependency for good. Others express a wish that they had done so but the addiction proved too strong to resist.

> At the age of 21 I was a married man with a family ... I was so proud, yet the gambling nearly always came first. At this time I used to gamble nearly every day of the week, whether it be horses, dogs or cards. Money was getting tighter and tighter yet it never stopped me gambling. Now the lies and deceit started. Me and my wife were always fighting about money ... I used to tell her lie after lie, and all for the sake of having a bet. She used to give me £10 or £20 to go and get the shopping. I never got there. I used to go straight into the bookies. I'd lose the money, go home and tell my wife some lie – it had either fallen out of my pocket on the way to the shops or something stupid like that. She'd never believe me and then the fighting would start. (Serving prisoner, aged 32)

However, this is also a stage at which the gambler, perhaps for the first time, finds it increasing difficult to ignore his or her destructive behaviour. It is, if you like, a forewarning of impending disaster that begins to filter through the cast iron wall of denial.

A downward spiral. Having been confronted with the consequence of their dependency, problem gamblers who are unable to face the mess will run away. This is often verbalised as having been done to avoid getting caught and punished for their aberrant behaviour but is, in reality, as much to do with their own fear of having to admit they are wrong and that they are not in control of their gambling.

> I started work at 16 and all the wages that I used to get would be squandered in the arcade. I used to take a lot of time off, and eventually I got the sack. I left home, and ended up sleeping on the streets. I eventually found somewhere to live – it was a hostel for homeless people. I then started to hang around with the wrong sort of people. I would go out stealing from cars and anything else I could get things from which I could sell in order to make money. I was often caught by the police and put into various hostels awaiting sentencing. However, I would run away and steal some

more. I stole thousands of pounds, and caused a great deal of damage because of my addiction to gambling. (Student, aged 20)

When problem gamblers stop running and have to find somewhere to rest it provides an opportunity for reflection. As the situation in which they find themselves is often worse than the one they have left (for example, walking away from the family home and into poor-quality rented accommodation) it is for some that crucial point of 'rock bottom'.

Total take-over. The elevation of gambling rapidly causes huge problems with relationships, work and day-to-day living in general. The semblance of having a conventional lifestyle begins to unravel. Lies have to be concocted to cover earlier lies and even the agile mind of the problem gambler starts to lose track of the duplicity. By this stage gambling has taken over the person's life to the total exclusion of everything else.

Gambling as in breathing, is our life blood. Waking hours are gambling hours either planning, anticipating or 'in action'. We become adept at excusing our lifestyle in as many ways as proves necessary to ensure we can stay 'at it'. Belief that we remain in control, can stop it as and when we want to or, worse, we no longer care as long as we can do as we like, are used as defensive counters to suggestions that we don't bet 'normally'. (Book-keeper, aged 52)

It is at this stage that the need to continue gambling is likely to block out all sense of decency and propriety. Close family, friends and employers are likely to suffer the same fate – that is, they become expendable in the face of the gambler's desperate need to get back to the 'action'.

Desperate deeds. For some gamblers the dependency drives them to desperate deeds. The desperation can be turned outwards or inwards. I recall a case some years ago where a young man in his twenties attempted to murder his mother. He had a loving and close relation-ship with her but the prospect of inheriting the house in which they lived proved too much of a temptation. The need for gambling money became overpowering and he became blind to the consequences of his actions. (As I write a Hampshire man has just been sentenced to life imprisonment for murdering his wife so that he could pay off his gambling debts with the insurance money.)

When the despair is turned inwards the gambler looks at suicide as a means of bringing the situation to an end. Whilst this can be construed as the ultimate selfish act there is no doubt that when the gambler actually faces the destruction the gambling has caused it can appear to be the only solution.

> I attempted suicide three times after I split up with my girlfriend – not because of her, but because I was gambling worse than ever. I didn't think I could stop, burgling again, conning people out of money. I was homeless no end of times due to gambling. (Mature student, aged 38)

When you talk to problem gamblers a great many of them will say that they contemplated murder as a means either of obtaining money or of avoiding discovery. Many more will say they thought about suicide to escape from the awful mess – a real reflection on the desperation problem gamblers can feel and the huge destruction it can cause the individual with a serious dependency on gambling.

The Effect on Family and Others

It has been suggested that as many as 15 other people are adversely affected by one adult problem gambler (Lesieur and Custer 1984), although for adolescents the figure is only likely to affect their immediate family and maybe a few friends (Griffiths 1995). It is not hard to imagine the emotional and material effect problem gambling can have on:

- *the gambler's partner*, in every aspect of his or her life
- *their children*, through emotional and material deprivation or inconsistency
- *the gambler's parent(s)*, both emotionally and materially
- *the partner's parent(s)*, who experience a conflict of loyalties, and who may be affected both emotionally and materially
- *the gambler's employer*, through erratic work, absenteeism and embezzlement
- *the gambler's work colleagues*, through missing money and the need to cover for the gambler's absences
- *the gambler's friends or relations*, from whom the gambler has 'borrowed', in addition to emotional conflict caused

- *small businesses*, owed money by the gambler but having to write off debts

Additionally, state agencies can become involved when the gambler is either prosecuted or convicted of crimes. The partner and family are, as a result of the misappropriation of money or lack of earned income, often forced to rely on state benefits. It is the partner and children of the gambler who are likely to bear the brunt of the destructive cycle of problem gambling. The following are likely to be some of the more harmful effects.

Broken promises. The gambler, in an effort to appease a disgruntled partner, may make promises such as going on holiday, shopping for the much-needed furniture or just having money available. When the time comes to keep the promise gamblers will have a ready excuse unless they have managed to win, borrow or retain sufficient money to carry out the promise. As the gambling increases, however, the list of broken promises will increase including, if the problem has become known, that of giving up gambling.

Money shortage. Lack of financial resources is an inevitable consequence on the family of a problem gambler and a cause of acute anxiety to the partner. Depending on the gambling activity a big win might produce enough to meet any debts and pay for a holiday. The shortages will very soon reappear as the gambler re-enters a losing phase. This uncertainty about money undermines the confidence of the partner as well as eroding the basis of trust within the relationship.

Debts. Debts are almost certain to accrue and it is quite likely that their extent is kept hidden from the partner. When they do find out that there is a large accumulation of debt it often comes as a great shock that further erodes confidence and undermines the relationship. It may also cause the partner increased strain in his or her other relationships if they feel obliged to approach family or friends for money or support. Fear is also a consequence of debt both from the point of view of people finding out and from the pressure of debt collectors. The family of the problem gambler begins to dread the knock at the door.

Absence from home. Being away for long periods outside the expected working hours is a huge cause of anxiety and mounting suspicion. The gambler may be shocked when accused of having an affair but is more likely to have an excuse ready. This would be supported by an emphatic denial of wrongdoing and reassurances of love and faithfulness to him or her. The partner, on the other hand, may be less convinced and begin to harbour a sense of having been betrayed.

Lying. Not telling the truth becomes the stock-in-trade of the problem gambler and when caught out will leave the partner feeling shattered. The realisation that the gambler is lying destroys the whole basis of trust and is likely to put a tremendous strain on the love between gambler and partner. The discovery that the gambler has been lying may simply bring the extent of the gambling into the open or it may prove to be the catalyst in the subsequent breakdown of the relationship. The emotional trauma experienced by the partner can be seriously damaging.

Social isolation. A falling-off in social contacts is a gradual process that is probably totally unapparent at the beginning of the relationship. One of the initial attractions of the gambler may have been their flamboyant or extrovert lifestyle, exciting visits to the casino or racetrack and a seemingly wide range of friends. It is all very superficial or may be a carefully constructed fabrication. As the money shortages bite, the gambler is increasingly absent, and the relationship becomes strewn with lying and broken promises, so the social isolation increases. This is likely to be due to a combination of the partner's own loss of self-esteem and confidence, the disillusion of friends who have been conned out of money or let down, and missed opportunities to socialise.

Loss of status. Reduced status arising from the social isolation, material shortage and strained personal relationship is likely to be a further consequence of problem gambling. This is exacerbated if the gambler loses their job, especially if this is a result of misconduct that becomes known within the local community. Yet again the confidence and emotional stability of the partner is likely to be seriously undermined.

Criminal activity. Illegal acts that have been perpetrated by the gambler and have been discovered can stigmatise the whole family. As a result they could well become ostracised by friends and acquaintances. Pressure may be put on the partner to abandon the criminal gambler. Occasionally it can be the partner who becomes involved in criminal activity, either as a means of redressing an acute financial crisis threatening the family, or as a form of collusion with the gambler in order to retain their love.

CASE HISTORY

Mick's self-history highlights some of the ways in which the individual gambler is affected:

I am 58 years old and although I have not gambled for a long period of time I have had a 'gambling problem' most of my life.

Looking back it started with regular family card games, particularly 'Newmarket'. Stakes were 1d (old money). It was the most exciting thing I can remember of my childhood. By the time I was 15 years old things changed. I had a paper round and saved up £12, a lot of money at the time. Then a fair arrived close to both where I lived and the post office. In just one week all the money had gone on a 1d 'Win or Lose' ball-bearing machine (in those days, 240d made £1). At the same period of time I started 'penny up the wall' at school. Despite getting good pocket money as well as earnings from the paper round I used to creep downstairs in the middle of the night to steal halfcrowns from my father's jacket.

I started work, pay day was Friday and so was West Ham dogs, so most Saturdays I was broke. Then they opened betting shops. I loved them ... They loved me ... I was making them rich. I soon realised the job I was in didn't pay enough for me to gamble because by now I had joined Charlie Chester's Casino.

If I had money, my typical day would be to leave a bet on the horses in the betting shop at lunchtime. If I won I'd go to the dogs in the evening and, if I won again, on to the casino. My trips to the dogs became fewer and my presence at the casino was very rare.

Work was easy to get at this time so my plan was to get jobs where I could see a 'fiddle'. I became a long-distance lorry driver, fiddling my fuel and night-out money, and stealing by selling the goods that I carried. All to have a bet. Before long I had a criminal record.

In 1970 I was sent to prison for 18 months, but this did not stop me from gambling. I gambled inside, got into trouble with debts and had to persuade my girlfriend to bail me out. On leaving prison I did what I had been doing for years, promised never to gamble again. For a short time (three months) it worked. My girlfriend and I worked hard, saved and got married. It was a large wedding, everything was paid for except the free drinks bar in the evening. I had gambled that day so my saviour this time was my best man.

I was out of trouble again. The marriage lasted one year. Remarkable considering that on pay day I would finish work, go to the pub and play cards all night. Not only did I go home with no money but with someone in the 'school'. The bills soon mounted and that was that. Did I change? Did I hell. I got worse, gambling was all I needed in life.

More relationships, flats and credit cards followed until in 1983 a friend persuaded me to go into partnership in an engineering business. He knew of my gambling but also knew all gamblers are hard-working, they have to be to feed the habit.

In 1985 I remarried, for security, a widow with four grown-up sons, own house, and everything paid for. I drove her to alcoholism and, not knowing I was the root cause I went to an AA meeting to 'support' her.

Despite my gambling the business went well, dealing with many national and international companies. In 1989/90 two major things happened. My gambling luck was worse than usual and I drastically under-quoted a large contract. A High Court Sheriff appeared at our office wanting £10,000. I had a breathing space of two days before everything would come to light.

On the Monday I left the marital bed like a sneaky little rat, quietly taking as much clothing as I could and not waking the wife. For the next 58 days I travelled the country in a van kitted out for good living with bed, cooker and TV. I travelled over 5000 miles backwards and forwards so as not to be traced and continued heavy gambling until the money ran out.

I now had four options: sleep rough and go on the dole; kill myself; return home and be killed by my business partner; or go to prison and be protected. I chose option four. I handed myself in and was arrested. In court the next day I broke down and asked for help with my gambling problem (the first time I admitted I had a problem).

The Effect on Children

The effect of problem gambling on children within the family is as destructive as that on a partner and in many instances will scar them for life. I have constructed the following from a seminar that took place during a Gamblers Anonymous

Convention in 1994 that I attended. Gamblers, their partners and their children spoke movingly of the pain and trauma they had experienced as a result of problem gambling.

Family experience of money shortages, long absences by the gambler, threatening telephone calls or visits by creditors, arguments and a strained atmosphere will cause tension and anxiety throughout the family.

Effect. However well the parents may feel that they have kept these problems secret, children are quick to pick up feelings and attitudes. They may themselves feel responsible for the unhappiness in the home, and for the failure and shortcomings of a parent. It is quite possible that when the real reason for the dysfunction is kept from them the children begin to believe that they are to blame – especially when they feel neglected by both parents.

A need for attention is felt by the children within the gambler's family. To overcome this feeling of neglect or lack of affection by one or both parents a child is likely either to emulate the role and personality of one parent or seek a substitute for affection elsewhere.

Effect. If it is the father who is the gambler it is a son who is likely to become a gambler in order to win attention by sharing his dad's interest. When the natural affinity lies with the opposite-gender parent it is likely to be the daughter who develops the interest in gambling. Alternatively, the children might adopt the same attitude displayed by the non-gambling partner and become martyrs, mothers or malcontents (see Chapter 12).

Collusion is demanded from the children by either the gambler or the non-gambling partner. This will usually take the form of being asked to keep secrets from the other parent, thereby making them unwilling accomplices in the web of lies and deceit.

Effect. This can split the children's loyalties, force them to keep secrets and, when challenged, to lie against their better judgement. Furthermore, it is likely to inculcate an adult role model that is based on avoiding or hiding the truth.

Inappropriate roles can be ascribed to children within the dysfunction of a problem gambler's family. One or more of them may have to take on adult responsibilities far earlier than they should. They may have to face ridicule, taunts or threats from their own peer group. The non-gambling partner, unable to rely on his or her partner for emotional support may turn to a child of the family to provide an emotional prop.

Effect. This is likely to cause children considerable role confusion and to be a source of much unhappiness for them. They may have the traumatically difficult balance to achieve between split loyalties and taking on responsibility for a parent at the expense of their own natural progression through childhood.

Traumatic events that could have been avoided become part of the children's lives. These may include heavy demands for money from creditors accompanied by threats to their parents or to themselves; receiving a gift from their gambling parent only to find it has been taken back again a few days later; having to go without and consequently struggle for status within their peer group because of straitened circumstances; being hastily looked after by a relative, whom they may or may not like, so as to be kept from knowing their parent has disappeared, been arrested, or is faced with some other deeply negative experience.

Effect. The children may well grow up feeling excluded and not trusted by their parents. If they are not informed they can imagine all sorts of terrifying possibilities, feel guilty, and go into a process of grieving at having lost that parent.

Being shielded from the truth, either the full extent of the gambling or the consequences of it, can particularly be the case when the parent(s) want to protect the children from the fact that serious crimes committed by Mum or Dad have been exposed. The children are lied to by one or both of them to cover up the fact that their father or mother is consequently facing prosecution or is in prison. Elaborate plans are made to give the impression that the gambling parent is working away from home.

Effect. This cover-up is very much concerned with the parents' inability to cope with the shame of the situation rather than protecting the children. But the children will feel let down, will instinctively know something is wrong, and will be bewildered that they cannot see the absent parent. Should the children be told later, or worse still, find out from a source outside the family, it will be a severe traumatic shock, invoking feelings of anger, sadness, guilt and lack of self-worth.

SUMMARY

A severe problem gambler will spend the whole of his or her waking life involved with the activity. The effect of a serious dependency on gambling has devastating consequences for the individual concerned as it encroaches upon every aspect of their life and drives them to a destructive and secretive lifestyle. The effect on the family is likely to be equally damaging in terms of material well-being, broken trust and impaired relationships.

CHECKLIST

Some of the principal effects of a gambling dependency on the individual and on family members are listed below.

The Problem Gambler

An individual held within the grip of a gambling dependency is likely to experience some or all of the following effects:

- Deceptive or deviant behaviour.
- Cheating and stealing from family, friends and employers.
- The development of a self-centred lifestyle.
- Living in a trance-like state.
- Causing hardship and heartache to others.
- A downward spiral in both behaviour and standard of living.
- Being totally controlled by the need to gamble.
- Contemplation or the carrying out of acts of desperation on self or others.

The Partner or Parent

The person closest to the problem gambler is also strongly adversely affected by his or her behaviour. They are undermined by:

- Unkept promises.
- Constant money shortages.

- The accumulation of debt.

- The gambler's long absences from home.

- The gambler's avoidance of responsibility.

- Persistent and repeated lying.

- Social isolation from family and friends.

- Loss of standing within the local community.

- Exposure of the gambler's criminal behaviour.

- Personal feelings of failure and disillusionment.

The Children of the Problem Gambler

The effect on children is as destructive, if not more so, as that on others who might be involved. They are likely to suffer from:

- Neglect by one or both parents.

- A lack of affection by their parent(s).

- A need to follow the gambling parent's interest to receive attention.

- Split loyalties.

- Having to lie and keep secrets inappropriately.

- Having the truth kept from them.

- Being used by a parent as a substitute adult or emotional prop.

- An undue amount of trauma being experienced during their childhood.

- A lack of self-confidence.

- Feelings of misplaced guilt.

7 Asking for Help

*I realised I had a problem when my firm gave me the sack
when they discovered I was stealing from them.
My world just fell apart and, for the first time, I realised
I needed help.*

(Fred – former insurance salesman, aged 35)

It has to be realised that gamblers don't see their obsession with the machine, the betting office or casino as a problem. Obtaining money to gamble or to pay off debts may be difficult but, in the mind of the gambler, these are caused by external circumstances and not by their own behaviour. Similarly, the strained and broken relationships are not their fault, but rather a failure by the other person to understand.

This denial of responsibility stems from the driving force that makes gambling more important than anything else in their life. When a real crisis is reached and the extent of their gambling is discovered this denial becomes harder to sustain. For some it is a point at which they can break through the defensive wall they have constructed and face their behaviour. However, others are just as likely to react by fleeing the situation or wriggling out of it by promising anything in order to reduce the pressure. These promises are often meaningless as they are simply a device for buying more time and manipulating the situation so that gambling can be resumed as soon as possible. In the words of Gordon Moody:

It is well known that rock bottom for one is three-quarters or half-way down for another. Apart from suicide, there seems to be no absolute bottom, no place where you absolutely must stop, no point where the only way is upwards. There are, however, ledges on the way down. Previously, we have called them crises. Hit one of those and you are temporarily halted, you suffer shock, pain, alarm, desperation. If you make no sense of it but turn and run, or try to scheme your way out of it, you are off the ledge and falling again. Any ledge, though can provide a rock bottom experience, provided that, as well as feeling the pain, you see that there is a way up. Indeed, you must see that up is the way and that you must take it. (Moody 1990, p. 40)

Gauging the genuineness of problem gamblers' motivation to change their lifestyle is far from easy. Deep-seated denial and a highly developed ability to manipulate the situation contribute to the difficulty in judging whether the desire to change is superficial or sincere. Nevertheless, there are a number of opportunities which should encourage those associated with the gambler to investigate whether there is a serious intention on the part of the gambler to look at their gambling behaviour.

When the Gambler Has Had Enough

Whilst it will usually be a crisis situation that provides a window of opportunity for gamblers to be confronted with their behaviour, they may also come naturally to that conclusion themselves as they become sickened by the vicious circle in which they have become trapped.

In this circumstance they may well ask for help directly or indirectly, at which point a positive and supportive response from those closest to the gambler is likely to provide further encouragement.

Gambling Environment as a 'Second Home'

Whilst some gamblers keep their activity a closely guarded secret, many others openly share the fact that they spend leisure time in amusement arcades, at bingo clubs, in the betting office or at the casino. If it becomes clear that the gambler is spending more time at these venues or is reluctant to account for time away, it is worth checking how comfortable they feel about this. It may be that they are happy with the situation as their preferred gambling environment meets their needs. On the other hand it may provoke discussion as to why they are spending more time gambling, how it is affecting other people and whether the gambler would like to reduce their gambling sessions. It is also likely that such a discussion could become linked to spending patterns. Quite clearly this is a sensitive area and the individual who is to approach the gambler on this issue will need to be aware of the possible repercussions. The value is that it provides the gambler with an opportunity to reflect on the way their life is changing at a point before it becomes a crisis.

Money Matters

Disagreements over money are the 'jagged rocks' of so many relation-ship break-ups whether gambling is involved or not. Where problem gambling is involved, financial difficulties are certain to be felt not only by the gambler but also by those around them. It is very tempting, as a means of avoiding conflict, to attribute financial difficulties to external factors and to shield the gambler from responsibility. Unfortunately this sort of collusion by a partner is well known in providing reinforcement of the gambler's distorted sense of achievement. Success is measured by the problem gambler in being able to stave off financial disaster by whatever means, and continuing to have money with which to gamble. On the other hand, relating the shortage of money to gambling and endeavouring to discuss the financial implications of this will at least cause the gambler to think about what they are doing. It should be borne in mind that the problem gambler is likely to have a second (secret) pile of money, so it may be helpful to let them know in a non-threatening way that money problems exist. Such an approach may lead to a revelation about the extent of debt which, whilst it might be a shock, could also precipitate the gambler into changing their behaviour.

Lies Uncovered

As the problem develops so the lying increases. A stage is usually reached where those close to the gambler become deeply suspicious of what they are being told, or they expose an absolute lie. Again, there is a temptation to make excuses for the gambler especially when they are able to turn the situation round to make it appear that they only lied to protect someone else. In doing so an opportunity may be lost to focus on the real reason for the lying and to put the responsibility back to the gambler. There is a risk that this may lead to further denial and greater secretiveness. But as the gambler is likely to be feeling bad about their deceit it also provides them with an opportunity to get off the merry-go-round of lying and to seriously consider the effect of their gambling.

Dwindling Circle of Friends

Concentration on gambling in preference to anything else and acute financial difficulties combine to weaken friendship ties. Inevitably this will feature in discussions and rows within the family. It is likely that the gambler will avoid or deny that a cause of this is the preoccupation with gambling. Reflecting back that this may be a contributory cause and reminding the gambler of the value of friendship links is a further means by which to make holes in their wall of denial.

Whilst these opportunities may cause problem gamblers to pause in their headlong flight to destruction, sadly, in many instances, it will not be enough to motivate them into changing their way of life. For some, they will never be deterred, and for others, they will go on until they perceive a real point of crisis in their lives – that hard and lonely rock bottom.

> I took stock. My wife and family didn't want anything more to do with me, later that day I was to become homeless, and I had no friends left who would help. I was scared and wanted to run again but something inside screamed 'enough'. Instead I asked to see my manager and told her everything … the first time I had admitted to anyone I had a problem with gambling. I knew I needed help. (Paul – sales executive, aged 45).

Losing a Relationship

> I had a good wife, a nice house, money in the bank and a decent job. I didn't need to gamble but I did. So again began the lies, deceit and the loss of trust from my wife and family … I lost my wife! I was separated from my two children and eventually left my job because of the depression I was suffering because of my loss. (Steve – hotel manager, aged 36)

Many problem gamblers feel the need for a significant relationship despite the fact that they find it impossible to trust another person. Their personality and lifestyle give them a quality that is attractive to their partners who, until they discover the fabrication, (naively) trust them. Exposure of the destruction caused by their gambling can come as a complete shock and severely undermine the trust the partner or family member had invested in the gambler. It also may shake gamblers out of their complacency as they go into overdrive to limit the damage. It can also prove to be a catalyst as the combination of fear and relief forces them to make a painful decision. The fear of losing someone dear to them and consequently having their inner feelings of failure magnified is enough to drive gamblers back to the activity in order to escape the pain. On the other hand it can provide the spur to change, especially when they feel they can let the pretence go. Problem gamblers who have chosen this latter course talk of the immense relief felt when they could stop the lying and deception. Talking through the consequences of their obsession with gambling and gaining the support of their partner or family member in tackling the dependency is a crucial first step in coming to terms with the situation.

Crime Discovered

> By now I was in deep trouble, I'd lost every penny I had and didn't
> have my monthly payment for the money-lenders. They came
> looking for me threatening to blow my legs off if I didn't pay them.
> So I did a stupid thing, I committed a robbery, got caught and am
> now in prison ... What a waste, my wife and children are paying for
> my mistakes but are sticking by me. Now I am in prison I am doing
> something about my gambling. (Peter – serving prisoner, aged 40)

Peter's story is not unusual in that in wasn't the money he needed to
gamble that led him into serious crime, it was the pressure of having
to repay debt. The urgency of this situation blinds gamblers into
crossing a line that, by the lies and deceit they have perpetrated on
family and friends, is already blurred. For some it is the first foray into
crime that provokes an internal crisis of conscience but for most the
anti-social behaviour continues until they are caught.

With a young problem gambler, in particular, resorting to crime is
likely to start with stealing from Mum's purse, Dad's credit card, or a
sibling's treasures. My experience over a number of years suggests that
for many families discovery of this criminality is the first indication
they have that a son or daughter is a problem gambler. It is, indeed, a
point of crisis for the whole family that is played out amidst high
emotions. It is also a point at which the young gambler is susceptible
to change as there is often a genuine motivation to look at themselves,
even if it is initially driven by the fear of punishment.

That fear of punishment for any problem gambler is magnified when
the crime has been committed outside the family circle. In many
instances, especially when the crime is that of embezzlement or stealing
from their business partner, the sums involved are spectacularly large.
Consequently, the sentence of the court is likely to entail imprisonment
which, while it satisfies the need to punish in relation to the seriousness
of the offence, does little to encourage gamblers to face up to their responsibilities. Insulated from the pressures and problems of everyday life,
once gamblers have adjusted to prison culture, they can carry on
gambling whilst 'inside' and avoid facing up to the situation.

However, it is a real point of crisis, especially when the crime is
discovered and the gambler cannot avoid being confronted by their
mistakes. It is a time when the gambler will promise to change. It is
wise to be cautious about these promises as, in my experience in
dealing with people facing court appearances, it can simply represent
another 'con' trick to avoid punishment. On the other hand the

discovery of serious crime enables gamblers to slough off the burden of their dependency. Having lost face and felt the intense humiliation that they had desperately tried to avoid, they can use the experience as a turning point without suffering further loss of self-esteem. It is a time when an assertive partner can take control of the situation and encourage the gambler to change. Even if some of the gambler's motivation is driven by a need to reduce the severity of punishment, supporting a serious endeavour to stop gambling at this time can create a real foundation for change.

The Debt Mountain

> Over the next few years I gambled nearly every day, piling up a skyscraper of debt. When my wife found out and we totalled it all up, the accumulation of what I owed from ten credit cards, bank overdrafts, a second mortgage on the house and the money I had secretly borrowed from her father, it came to over £90,000. I was devastated. I just sat at the table and cried, vowing that I would never gamble again. (Accountant, aged 50)

The first reaction of a problem gambler to the pressure of meeting a debt is to talk someone into lending them money, to misappropriate money to which they have access, or to steal. The second reaction is to stake the amount gained to win a larger amount. The third reaction may be elation should the gamble pay off but, more often than not, despair as they lose it all and proportionately increase what they owe.

The vicious circle continues until the possibility of discovery drives them either to undertake greater risks in an attempt to cover the debt or to run away. Eventually the debt situation gets so large and unmanageable that is cannot remain hidden, or the extent of the increasingly desperate criminality is exposed.

These are points of real crisis which can cause a reaction of genuine despair from gamblers and those who are close to them. As we will discover in a later chapter it is a necessary first step to bring a sense of order to a chaotic debt situation before anything else can be addressed. Whilst responsibility for the debt must remain with the gambler, managing the situation so that repayments can be coped with can again provide the catalyst that induces a genuine desire to change.

Homelessness

> I was wet, cold and miserable as I thought about my mad panic to leave my flat and get away from Jock's threat to kill me if I didn't

repay £20,000 by today. It was odd I felt safe the other end of the country when I was penniless, homeless and in deep trouble. (Former stockbroker)

A number of gamblers I have spoken with, who had built up large debts with money-lenders or business partners, saw running away as the only way out of the situation. In some cases they have left behind a spouse or partner to face angry creditors or to find the money themselves because the gambler had duped them into signing as guarantor. Having time and again obtained money to cover a part of a debt, the gamblers' myopic belief that they will win more has lured them back into the betting office or casino – usually with disastrous results. Denial by running away appears as the simple solution. The problem will disappear, the past can be blocked out, and the gambler will feel free to start all over again. When they are left homeless, however, because of running away or perhaps because their spouse has thrown them out, it becomes more difficult to continue the denial of responsibility. It is a time when the gambler is particularly receptive to the need to seek help. The turning-point in many stories I have heard comes when gamblers find themselves in a hostel, perhaps awaiting a court appearance or, when in 'mid-flight' they have had a chance encounter with a person or maybe some visual image that makes them stop and think.

Lost Control

As usual I had set out with such hope that I only bought a one-way train ticket. I was convinced that I would be able to travel home in style by taxi. As I trudged home through the dark London streets without a penny wondering how I was going to explain to my wife why they were going to foreclose the mortgage, I knew I'd had enough and that my life was out of control. (Steven – travel agent, aged 40)

The number of problem gamblers who reach this point and subsequently sort out their lives by themselves is unknown. In my experience of gambling helplines, however, the self-disgust and loss of personal or professional status can override the instinct to carry on denying there is a problem. The urge to gamble may be as strong as ever but a growing desire to change causes them to seek help. The initial response to this cry for help is crucial in encouraging the gambler's motivation.

CASE HISTORY

This case history written by Phil in 1998 covers some of the issues raised in this chapter.

> I was born in the 1960s and until my teenage years gambling played hardly any role in my life. However, it was on the fringe via seaside amusements and cards at school. I left school with the usual quota of exams: eight O-levels and one A-level (intelligence is no advantage to the total life of gambling).
>
> By the time I was 17 I had started to frequently gamble via pub fruit machines and town arcades. Arcades are strangely labelled 'amusements'; strange because when I've been in them (and I've spent literally days in there), there is seldom any amusement amongst the ranks of button pushers – just a frowning concentration feeding the hungry slots, until at last pockets are emptied. As they always are!
>
> Early in the 1980s I was on the dole (one of Maggie's rejects!) and my gambling began to affect my whole life; borrowing, lying, cheating, stealing, anything to chase those magic lights and elusive nudges. My parents often bailed me out of trouble and somehow I abided by the law. The periodic bouts of family despair were typified when I was once given some money to buy some new shoes I'd wanted and whilst in town I proceeded to gamble the whole amount in a very short time; eventually ringing home (reversing the charge) as darkness fell to be picked up by my parents like a dog with its tail between its legs.
>
> However, in late 1983 I got a job with the civil service (cheers Maggie) but the cloud on the horizon was the bookmaker. A few months later I was introduced to the furtive world of the bookies; again, a place of hollow-eyed despair as the punters scan the newspapers for that one SURE THING. For the next few years my gambling knew no bounds. Huge debts, loans, selling my car, credit cards – all were swallowed up in my insatiable gambling frenzy. Until by 1987 I decided to embark on the greatest gamble of them all – serious crime in the shape of building society robbery.
>
> I am currently in prison serving a long sentence. The bulk of my offences have been robberies to gain money, which I promptly gambled away.
>
> Now, I often read of people who choose serious crime to finance

gambling habits and gambling is an addiction that reaches into all areas of the social strata. Recently, I have seen a case of murder, serious fraud by a policeman and numerous solicitors and accountants in court citing gambling as an excuse.

Yes, it's an addiction, but something I've eventually overcome. I gambled in prison as well. Until in 1995 I finally realised the blindingly obvious; that gambling and me are a chemical mix which made nuclear fallout seem like a dose of the flu compared to the mayhem I'd wrought on the lives of others and on myself.

Now in my thirties, I can grasp some perspective at last. I realise that I must try to help the many compulsive gamblers out there. I've become a Christian believer and have maintained my 'new life' existence.

Responding to the Cry for Help

The reason why the response to a cry for help is of such paramount importance is that the low self-esteem of the gambler is, at this vulnerable time, likely to be in shreds. In my view this is a time for giving as much positive reinforcement as possible.

Whilst they may admit that their actions have caused a problem there is often a natural tendency to minimise the extent of this. Interestingly, I have seen the reverse of this with a group of problem gamblers whose competitive nature got the better of them and they tried to outdo each other with tales of destruction.

As a starting point it is useful for gamblers to ask themselves the questions outlined in Chapter 3 which can provide a useful indication as to the extent to which gambling has taken over their life.

The first feeling mentioned by gamblers when they at last face up to the fact that it is a real problem is that of relief. The vortex of finding money to gamble, anticipation, the action, and crashing down again, stops. Gamblers talk of an overwhelming sense of release from the need to kept it all a secret and freedom from the daily web of deceit. For some these feelings rush upon them almost immediately and for others the relief is a slower process.

There are a number of steps that gamblers and those close to them can take, once they have come to the decision that they need help.

Ask for help. The first small but significant step the gambler takes is to ask for help. They may speak to their partner or other family member, their employer, the police, a caring agency, or by contacting a specialist helping agency such as GamCare (see Chapter 14) or

Gambler's Anonymous (see Chapter 10). Asking for help also applies to the family as they find coping with the pain alone an unbearable experience. Taking this step is not easy as there is stigma and shame attached to the devastation caused by problem gambling. The family members, however, also need support to get them through a traumatic time of change and readjustment.

Be honest. It is absolutely vital that gamblers enter a process of wanting to change by being honest with themselves. Problem gamblers are good confidence tricksters but they also con themselves into thinking that they are different and special and that the horse that they have selected will win the next race. Instead they need to believe they are similar to the rest of the population with strengths and weaknesses and that they have no special relationship with Lady Luck. They also need to be honest with other people, however painful this may be to achieve. Having spent years constructing falsehoods they can begin the painstaking process of re-building trust with others. The family members should examine their own honesty as well, as they may have in part been responsible for, encouraged or colluded with the gambler.

Recognise the seriousness of the problem. Whilst it is likely that the gambler will have a shrewd idea of how serious their obsession is, the family members may not. It has to be recognised that the gambler cannot simply 'give it up' without considerable help and support. It also has to be recognised that the gambler has got so heavily involved because it is meeting some deep need. They like the feelings that they get whilst gambling and probably it can, or has, given them a 'high' like nothing else in their lives.

Deal with debts. I have already suggested that the majority of problem gamblers ask for help when debts can no longer be sustained and the repercussions of owing money threaten to expose them. It is very difficult to concentrate on putting your life back together when the need to repay a debt appears as a falling Sword of Damocles. Whilst the extent of money owed can indeed be huge, creating order out of a chaotic debt situation can quickly bring matters back into manageable proportion. Making an inventory of *all* the debts and then seeking early help from a specialist debt counselling service such as that run by the Citizens' Advice Bureau, is likely to prove very beneficial.

Talk. Sharing how they feel when they gamble, what triggers them into wanting urgently to return to the fruit machine, bookies or casino and why it makes them feel good is a further early response to asking for help. Gamblers may have no insight as to what drives them and are likely to have bottled it up for years. Just talking about it to someone who will listen in a non-judgemental fashion can open the door to understanding and future prevention strategies. This is an important role for the family member who should respond by actively listening to what the gambler is saying – not interrupt but, perhaps, make mental or written notes about salient points. The gambler should be encouraged to talk as openly and honestly as possible.

Abstain. I have always had doubts about the notion that only by abstaining from gambling for the rest of their lives will the gambler be 'cured', as this is an avoidance technique rather than behaviour adaptation. However, I do not discount the fact for older gamblers where gambling has become an ingrained aspect of their lives it may be an appropriate strategy. For the young problem gambler whose adult life is only just beginning such an exhortation can appear meaningless. However, for the problem gambler seeking help to break the dependency a period of total abstinence does make a great deal of sense because it lays down a clear yardstick beyond which the rest of their life can be constructed.

One day at a time. This self-help maxim is one for us all, as when life is really tough it is better to look at where we are putting our feet than scanning the horizon. The perspective becomes manageable, the target realistic: 'Just for today, I will not gamble' is an excellent self- help strategy for the problem gambler.

Keep a record. Keeping a record of progress provides a visual image of the length of time the individual has remained gambling free. This simple yet effective notation on a calendar or in a diary helps boost confidence and gives a measure of success.

Be positive. The tendency, when gamblers cannot resist the urge to gamble again, is for them to become entirely negative and throw in the towel. This defeatist attitude is not constructive and does not reflect the energy required for change. Reference to the daily record can reinforce how they have done *and* set a target to beat. So instead of giving in, gamblers can respond to their competitive streak with the determination to stop for a longer period than before.

Be clear on responsibility. It is difficult for gamblers to accept responsibility for their behaviour when they have spent years avoiding it. However, the self-reward for taking back responsibility can do much to improve confidence. The gambler should avoid asking others to collude in any way. It is the gambler's responsibility not to return to gambling and in accepting that it was their behaviour that caused the problem. The family members must guard against colluding with the gambler. It is something they may have done consciously or sub-consciously for years and, in their way, they have encouraged the gambling. Attempts by the gambler to transfer guilt inappropriately should also be resisted. Responsibility for the gambling lies firmly at the door of the gambler but responsibility for change lies with the family members as well.

Self-reward. A further positive stroke that can reinforce the problem gambler who is seeking help to change again comes from within. I would suggest that after a couple of gambling-free weeks recovering problem gamblers should go out and buy something for themselves such as an item of clothing, jewellery, and so on. This may well be something they have not been able to do for years as all their money has gone into the 'gambling pot'. This self-reward system should take place even if the gambler is trying to pay off large debts. Feeling good about themselves is vital to their recovery.

Love and respect. Whilst trust will take time to be rebuilt, when a parent or partner loves the gambler that message needs to be communicated. The gambler who may have dismissed any notion that they are loved, equally should accept expressions of love, affection and respect. For everyone in life self-esteem is a fragile part of our personality and for the gambler it is particularly so. It is therefore of great importance to know that despite what has happened, and despite tough decisions that have to be made, they are still loved.

Managing money. Many gamblers have said that it has been a great help in the early stages of change if someone has managed their money for a while. This is a natural role for a close family member and, indeed, may be essential in sorting out the repayment of debt. If this strategy is under-taken everyone concerned must approach it with honesty. Also it should be agreed at the outset that it will only happen for a finite period of time and then be reviewed. Sooner or later it is important that gamblers take back responsibility for their own financial affairs ... yet another step in helping them to feel good about themselves.

Encouraging other interests. As gambling will have taken up a large slice of the individual's life it is also important to fill the void created when gambling stops. If the gambler is still in a family situation, greater involvement in the life of the family provides a ready answer. Even in a busy life it will be important that time is found for the gambler to develop, together with other family members, a range of interests. As mentioned earlier in the book I have discovered that many gamblers were, in the past, particularly good at a sport or had a specific interest. When the gambling ceases it is very useful to look at how these interests can be revived and/or new ones developed. Constructing several interests rather than plunging headlong into one will of course reduce the chance for the dependency to re-emerge in something else.

SUMMARY

The most likely time that problem gamblers will seek help is when they experience a real crisis. Until that time they will strongly deny they have a problem, probably even to themselves, and will blame their misfortune on other people or external influences. The crisis or 'rock bottom' that triggers acknowledgement that their gambling is a problem can be precipitated by many different situations. It more commonly occurs when the gambler can no longer avoid being confronted with their behaviour. When this point is reached there are a number of steps that the gambler can take to address their dependency and to begin the process of change.

CHECKLIST

Situations that provide an opportunity to help the gambler focus on their need to change include:

- **Acceptance by the gambler that control has been lost** – the step before they ask for help.

- **When they ask for help**, having realised for themselves that gambling has taken control of their lives.

- **An observation that too much time is being spent in the gambling environment**, which can provoke discussion as to how this is affecting the life of the gambler and others.

- **The stresses and strains of money matters**, which are bound to be a recurring point of family discussion.

- **Lies uncovered**, which will cause shock and anger but can lead to a hard look as to why.

- **A dwindling friendship circle,** which is likely to cause stress but can focus discussion on interests and needs.

- **Losing a close relationship,** which is likely to bring a painful opportunity for the gambler to seriously reflect on their own behaviour.

- **A crime discovered** – a point of real crisis that is likely to present stark choices.

- **Facing a mountain of debt,** which can appear insurmountable yet can also be the catalyst for co-operation and compromise.

- **Homelessness** – a time of fear for the gambler, but a situation that forces reflection.

A positive response to the cry for help is vital in enabling the gambler to take further steps towards addressing the dependency. They should be encouraged to:

- Be honest with themselves and others.

- Deal with debts.

- Accept responsibility for their gambling.

- Abstain from gambling whilst breaking the dependency.

- Talk about how gambling makes them feel.

- Take one day at a time.

- Keep a record of 'gambling-free' days.

- Be positive and not to give up after a lapse.

- Reward themselves after a gambling-free period.

- Develop alternative interests.

8   The Telephone Helpline

*That's the good thing, it is good to know that when I need it
I can just pick up the phone and talk to someone –
it's problem solved.*

(Helpline caller addicted to betting)

The telephone is a form of communication that lends itself to the human need to talk through a personal situation. As far as I have been able to ascertain the first official telephone helpline established in the UK was that of the Samaritans. It is also probably the best-known helpline, providing as it does a channel of hope for those who are suicidal, despairing, depressed or lonely. It was as a volunteer helper with this service, started in 1953 by the Reverend Chad Varah in the Crypt of St Stephen's Church, Walbrook, London, that I first learnt the healing power of the telephone helpline.

There are a number of factors that contribute to its ability to help those that are troubled. The following are some of the more important ones.

It requires the caller actively to make the first move. Whether driven by despair, threat, fear or curiosity, it is the caller who makes the first contact. This step is very significant as it requires an active effort, both mental and physical, to call a helpline. For many it is a vital first step back from a situation that is out of control or has overwhelmed them. In the early stages of a call this is sometimes the only positive aspect in a sea of deep, dark negativity.

Control rests with the caller. At any time during the telephone conversation it is within the caller's control to terminate the call. That this can be done instantly and decisively is an important safety mechanism when the pain of continuing becomes too much. More real control rests with the person asking for help than in almost any other counselling or advice situation.

The cloak of anonymity. Perhaps the most attractive aspect of the telephone helpline is that it enables the caller who wishes to do so, to remain anonymous. Whilst, in my experience over the years, most are quite content to offer at least their forename, many find the opportunity to remain completely anonymous the single most important factor that enables them to use the service. Intimate personal disclosures that have the potential to damage the caller are uttered within a short time on the line, freed by the knowledge that it is safe to unload the heavy weight of conscience.

Low-cost commitment. Telephone helplines are mainly 'free-call' or 'lo-call' numbers that act as an encouragement not only to ring, but to spend time talking without the nagging fear of running up a big bill.

Taken on trust. Whilst it could be an erroneous notion, a helpline is, in the mind of the majority of callers, accorded an immediate status of being trustworthy. As we tend to think the best of people the logic is that the service is there to give the caller something at no gain to the helpline service. It is the blind trust of hope – which puts a huge onus of responsibility on the organisers of the helpline service.

Readily available. Although it may take time, or be by chance, after finding the number of the service the caller has easy access. It requires no travelling, no awkward registrations, no embarrassing face-to-face meetings. The generally wide span of hours a helpline is available provides convenience for the caller who can either ring the line as a spontaneous reaction or plan a time to call that suits their circumstances.

Instant relief. Having committed oneself to picking up the phone, within a few minutes the caller can experience a tangible sense of relief. For many it is the first time they have been able to talk to anybody about their situation. The initial opening is tentative but as soon as they feel able to trust the voice at the other end of the line the process of unburdening begins. I can recall many instances where callers have expressed amazement that they have just spoken of personal matters for the first time in their lives. Others break down in tears, in anger, or in sadness as the emotion of sharing their situation wells up and is freed by the power of the helpline call.

An effective counselling medium. Having established a link with which the caller feels comfortable the telephone can be used to conduct a series of pre-arranged conversations that provide effective counselling. Some of the advantages for the caller are that they are not restricted by location and can pick a specialist to work through their problem; there is greater equality in the client–counsellor relationship and the tradition that counselling takes place on the counsellor's terms is challenged; callers can feel safe to talk freely about deeply personal issues and emotions (Rosenfield 1997).

Helplines and Problem Gambling

The History of Gambling Helplines in the UK

From these opening remarks it is easy to see the value of a helpline to a person affected by a gambling dependency. As far as I know, the first specialised helpline in the UK for problem gamblers was set up in 1982 by Gamblers Anonymous (GA). This service, which is still available today, has traditionally been staffed by members of the GA fellowship and aims to encourage compulsive gamblers who ring to attend a GA meeting.

Following a Home Office report in 1988 (Graham 1988) that addressed concern about young gamblers becoming addicted to fruit machines, the trade organisation BACTA (British Amusement Catering Trades Association) set up its own helpline service. This was a courageous step as it was the first trade association to set up such a service. Unfortunately, no real thought was given to the expectations and requirements of an effective helpline and it had little practical value. Later the Association recognised this and sought the assistance of a commercial telephone counselling agency which, although not specialised, provided a degree of professionalism. More recently BACTA has been able to terminate its own line in favour of the new GamCare National Helpline (see later).

The other development which laid a foundation for the current national service was that provided by the UK Forum on Young People and Gambling. Limited resources prevented that charity establishing a proper helpline but from 1990 an advice line operated for young problem gamblers and their parents, and for practitioners working with them. Whilst I was involved in that advice service, we took a number of calls from older gamblers and it became apparent, as the climate of gambling changed, that a dedicated helpline was needed.

The reasons why GamCare (see Chapter 14) considered that such a service had to be developed were based on the following facts.

- No broad-based helpline for problem gamblers existed in a developing climate of approval and legitimisation of gambling.

- Both 'hard' and 'soft' forms of gambling were increasing in terms of new products and availability.

- Gamblers Anonymous had reported a 17 per cent increase in calls to its helpline in 1995 – the first full year after the introduction of the National Lottery.

- The UK Forum advice line, although only receiving a few hundred calls, witnessed a year-on-year increase following the launch of the Lottery.

- A growing number of counselling and caring agencies were asking where help was available in response to their contact with problem gambling issues.

- Caring agencies, the government and sections of the gaming industry were encouraging the setting-up of a national helpline.

- Resources to properly establish such a service were likely to be available.

Creating a Professional Service

A caller to any helpline should be able to expect that they will be treated with respect and that the person answering the call will be understanding, empathetic and professional. Because of the vulnerability of the caller this standard has particular significance in responding to a gambling dependency.

In using the GamCare experience as an example, the first step was to establish the feasibility of developing a national helpline. In my view it was important to be clear about the service required and that which the agency could actually provide. Policy considerations relevant to setting up the helpline included:

- whether there was sufficient evidence that there was a demand for the helpline

- assessing the adequacy of financial backing to set up and maintain a viable service

- whether the service should be just for those who felt they had a problem or whether it should include anyone affected by a gambling dependency

- deciding to have a telephone number that was standard charge, local call charge or free

- whether the service should open a single line or more than one, and the hours the helpline would be available

- whether to use paid employees, volunteers, or a mixture of both

- the standard of the process by which staff would be selected and trained, and the extent to which they would receive regular on-going supervision and further training

- the extent to which calls would be monitored and whether to include direct recording

- the means by which the quality of the service could be evaluated

- the extent to which basic statistics would be kept that could, when suitably anonymised, be used to provide important information

- the extent to which confidentiality could be preserved, what it actually meant in organisational terms, and how the caller would be informed of this policy

- whether the service would simply provide support or would also include the giving of information, advice or an element of counselling

- what back-up facilities would be offered by the agency providing the helpline and the extent of any referral service

The crucial element is of course the quality of the people staffing the helpline. Having decided to use volunteers we selected and trained candidates who had the following attributes:

- a good telephone manner

- a non-judgemental attitude

- good listening skills

- had knowledge of, or experience in working with, an addiction

- demonstrated an understanding of gambling dependency

The GamCare experience is, I have no doubt, little different from other agencies that set up a facility to address an aspect of human vulnerability – it attracts a wide range of people who wish to volunteer, including those that have had the problem themselves or who have been affected by it. The value of those who have had direct experience is that they can bring a depth of understanding that cannot be matched by someone who has not been in that situation. The danger is that they may be unable to separate their own experience and emotions from those of the caller. It is therefore of great importance to determine the extent to which the volunteer has moved on from their own dependency and is able to respond professionally rather than personally.

Receiving Calls

The service provided by the GamCare helpline is not just to listen, support, provide information and then refer. It has been designed to be much more proactive than that. Where appropriate, the person staffing the helpline may give advice, and in a few cases – especially when the caller rings on a second or subsequent occasion – an element of counselling is introduced.

When a problem gambler calls, the first few minutes are vital in setting the tone and in encouraging the caller to continue. Whilst every call is unique there is a pattern and an experienced volunteer should in most instances be able to guide the caller through a process. The following framework provides, in my opinion, a sound basis for responding to a helpline caller.

Be open. At the very beginning of the call both the caller and the volunteer will have anxieties. However, it is the caller who is likely to feel most vulnerable and will quite likely be poised to terminate the call if the feeling of exposure becomes too great. The response must therefore be sincere, welcoming and safe. This doesn't require a great number of words but whatever is said must radiate warmth and encourage the caller to continue.

This is the GamCare helpline, how may I help you?

My name is Paul. Would you like to talk about it?

Listen actively. Beginning and staying with 'where the caller is at' is at the core of providing a service that is able to meet the needs of those affected by a gambling dependency. To do that the volunteer needs to listen carefully and actively to what is being said. Intervention should only be made to further encourage the caller to keep talking or to refocus the conversation on gambling. Taking notes is a part of active listening as they can provide a picture from which reference can be made. It is likely that basic statistical information will emerge during this phase of the call. Missing bits of information can be asked for as part of the prompting or checked later.

Aha ... What type of gambling is causing the problem? ... Is it the debt that has you worried? ... How did that happen?

Check motivation. There are a number of reasons why someone is prompted to call the helpline. It may be out of desperation from their current situation; it could be a knee-jerk reaction having suddenly come across the number; they may ring after harbouring the number for some months, having needed time to build up the courage; it may be that the gambler, finding him- or herself in a crisis, calls as an appeasing gesture to reduce pressure from another source; or they may have been 'told' to ring. It is important to try and establish the reason for calling the helpline and, following on from that, the strength of the gambler's motivation to address their dependency. This needs to be established whether it is the gambler that calls or a call about the gambler.

It is particularly hard to work with a caller where their motivation to change is low, or they ring because someone else wants them to call. Over the years I have often been confronted by a reluctant young problem gambler speaking on the telephone because a parent has demanded they did so – and, on occasion, with that parent standing beside the young person whilst they make the call! The response to this situation would be to suggest it may be better to have a private conversation with the caller at another time, even if you are then confronted by the parent. When the caller is able to speak with you without another person listening the first step is to explore with them if they would find talking on the telephone of value to *them*.

Another common reason for calling is to alleviate an immediate crisis such as an enforced separation from the family or a forthcoming court appearance with the underlying threat of a prison sentence. In this scenario the gambler is likely to be still denying their culpability and blaming the crisis on other people and external events. It is valuable in this circumstance to accept they are still in denial and that the gambler may have little genuine motivation to address the problem. Keep in mind the need to stay with 'where they are at'. At this point their defence of denial is likely to be quite weak and they may subconsciously be looking for a disassociated person to break through the barrier. They should be encouraged to look at their part in creating the situation by prompting them to talk through the chain of events that led up to the crisis and gently probing those in which their gambling played a part.

> *What do you think are the reasons why your partner is threatening to leave you? ... How did such a big debt situation come about? ... How did your partner react when you told her you had gambled away the mortgage repayments? ... Looking back on it, do you think your gambling has contributed to current difficulties?*

Others, of course, will ring knowing their gambling is out of control and are hoping the call will provide a way out of the mess – an instant cure; just like their fantasy that a big gambling win will solve all their difficulties. Helping to strengthen their resolve and suggesting some possible ways forward is the key to focusing their motivation to change.

Checking the perceived level of motivation is also important when taking a call from a family member. Whether or not they wish to positively support the gambler to change and are prepared to change themselves should guide the response. If they wish to support the gambler, working at it together is likely to be effective, but if they are not prepared to do so they should be encouraged to think through the consequences of change for them.

Encourage change. Change is a scary business which for the fragile personality of the problem gambler can appear beyond their reach. In their career from social to problem gambling they have ignored a whole succession of warning signs in the drive to satisfy their needs at any cost. Gambling continues to make them feel good as well as providing the comfort of familiarity.

Having established that they do want to change it is important to encourage them to explore ways that they feel might work for them. In my experience they often do have ideas but may have been discouraged by previous failed attempts or by the obstacles involved in securing the change. It is necessary to listen to what they are saying and share with them possible reasons behind the need to gamble.

For example, take a 26-year-old machine gambler who appears to be primarily driven to gambling because of the buzz factor. It would be useful to explore with him what other activities he may have followed previously that also answered that need. As I have mentioned earlier (see Chapters 3 and 5) a large number of young fruit machine gamblers had been, or still were, good at a sport or physical activity. Assuming that this is the case with our example, encouraging him to look at possible ways of getting back into that sport can inculcate a sense of purpose and belief that they can do something different.

May I ask if you like sport? ... You must have been very good to get a trial for Arsenal, what made you give it up? ... And what happened to your gambling at that time? ... Some gamblers describe gambling as meeting similar needs to those they got from sport, do you think that is true in your case? ... Would you like to get back into football? ... How might you be able to do this?

It may not be easy but problem gamblers do possess a drive and determination – the skill lies in encouraging them to redirect their energy.

Reinforce the positive. We all thrive on positive reinforcement, and in the case of problem gamblers this commodity may well have been in short supply over the years. It is therefore of vital importance to emphasise those aspects and achievements which they can feel good about in their life. I can recall conversations where this has been difficult, especially when they are depressed or they feel so badly about themselves that they have an urge to reject the notion that there are any positives. Indeed, they may draw considerable comfort from the idea that they are bad and their life is entirely negative. They can then feel threatened by the suggestion that there is a positive aspect to their life. On the other hand many, having picked up the phone in bleak despair, have responded gratefully to a focus on their positive attributes.

> You said that a couple of years ago you gave up gambling for five months; that sounds like a good achievement – what prompted that? … So your daughter needed you and from what you say you gave her tremendous support during that difficult time. … Perhaps helping someone you care about brings the best out in you and maybe meets some of your needs. … Are there ways you can take on this role again?

Suggest self-help strategies. Whilst the telephone can provide a respite to the desperation they are feeling, when individuals affected by the gambling dependency put down the telephone they are once again alone with the problem and with churned-up feelings from talking on the helpline. The positive aura they may have experienced for a short while begins to fade. For those who express a desire to change their behaviour and articulate a motivation to stop gambling it is appropriate to encourage them to think of strategies that may be of help. Some callers will have attempted, with varying degrees of success, to resist the urge to gamble by avoiding venues, restricting the amount of money they take with them, or by enlisting the support of family and friends. Even if these strategies have only worked for a short period of time this should be encouraged if the caller feels comfortable with the idea of trying them again. Additionally, it may be useful to share with them the strategies outlined in Chapter 7.

> Have you thought of keeping a record of each day you don't gamble? … A mark in a diary or on a calendar is enough to keep a tally … OK, so you have a lapse, the tally might help you to move on, it gives you a target to aim at, something to beat.

It has been said to me by a caller that reinforcing this positive action only brings further failure into sharper relief. This is possibly true of a pathological gambler who is driven by the subconscious need to lose, but for most, I would suggest, giving them 'permission' to feel good about themselves helps create that foundation for real and permanent change. When I asked a gambler in his fifties whose career had been littered with destruction and degradation what was the single most important factor that enabled him to change, he said: 'For the first time I can remember, I feel good about myself.'

Provide information. It would be very wrong to implant the notion that the helpline can answer all their questions or provide a total package to break free of the gambling dependency. The value of this contact is to provide a point of first resort, to encourage the gambler or family member to take those first steps that will lead them away from the destructive nightmare. It may well lead to further calls to the helpline or to assessment for either telephone or face-to-face counselling.

Enabling callers to make an informed choice is also important, so they may need to be told about what avenues of help are available locally to them. Encouragement to contact Gamblers Anonymous (see Chapter 10) is one possibility but this service is not available everywhere and is not an approach that suits everyone. Similarly, there may be alternative local services that the caller can approach depending on availability and the circumstances of the gambler or their family.

Are you saying you would like to contact a local service about the problem? ... There is a Gamblers Anonymous meeting near you that meets on Tuesdays, alternatively I have the details of a local counselling service that may be able to help.

Clearly, the effective means of providing referral information is in having a strong and comprehensive network of providers who can be of help to those affected by a gambling dependency. The more knowledge the helpline volunteers have about available services, the more they can advise callers as to what is on offer. In many instances the caller may articulate a reluctance to try a particular service. It is very difficult to spot whether this is based on fear, denial or other reasons so the role of the helpline caller should be restricted to providing information and encouraging the caller to take some action.

Safe ending. Ending the call can provoke as much anxiety as at the beginning. Some callers may do so abruptly and some may be reluctant to sever this new-found link of hope. In all cases it is important to create a safe ending. During the call, the volunteer would have formed a mental picture about the caller, and the caller would similarly have done so about the volunteer – although this may be less well defined. It is important that the volunteer maintains respect for the caller's feelings and what has been said, and is aware of their own feelings and responses. The temptation to 'feel good' by asking the caller 'Has that been of help?' should be avoided. Contributions by the volunteer that help create a safe ending include:

- a check on the volunteer's own understanding of the caller's situation, of options and strategies discussed, of information requested or referral information given

- reinforcing positive experiences and feelings

- an offer of ongoing telephone contact

This last point is very important as it provides an option for the future, the control of which is entirely in the hands of the caller. In my experience many problem gamblers value the opportunity to ring the helpline whenever they feel the urge to gamble. Any helpline that operates for less than 24 hours of necessity limits this option, but it is nevertheless a powerful bolster for the gambler wanting to stop. Equally, family members can gain comfort from the fact that they can call again. The offer alone conveys a message that the caller has been valued and is not just 'a nuisance'. Many callers ring again to report progress – both those that are still struggling and those who have stopped – and in all cases providing a further opportunity to reinforce the positives and give further encouragement.

The experience of the GamCare helpline indicates that the average length of time for a call with someone affected by a gambling dependency is around 25 minutes. In keeping with most counselling sessions I would recommend that no call should last beyond one hour. By focusing on the points listed above the volunteer should be able to guide a call to its conclusion. However, this is a skill that may take time to develop and it will be found that it is easier to achieve with some callers than others. It is helpful to establish early on in the call whether the caller has time to talk as many will indicate a natural limit because of other factors in their day. What is said, inflections of voice, the progress of the call, and reaching a natural break, are all indicative signs that can cue the volunteer, and help make it a safe ending.

We have talked about a great deal this morning ... the steps you have taken to stop sound really good, and your positive attitude comes across clearly. If you feel it will help do call again especially if you are feeling under pressure to gamble again and to share your progress.

SUMMARY

The first telephone helpline in the UK is thought to be that of the Samaritans. It is a very positive medium that helps an individual to talk through a troubling or personal situation. Contributing to this is the fact that control rests with the caller, it is an easily accessible service, and it can be an effective means of counselling. Care needs to be exercised in setting up a helpline for problem gamblers. The national helpline run by the National Association for Gambling Care, Educational Resources and Training (GamCare), provides a model of a structured service that reassures, encourages and supports the caller and, where appropriate, involves an element of counselling.

CHECKLIST

Problem Gambling Helpline: A Beneficial Service

There are a number of factors that contribute to a helpline providing a beneficial service for those affected by a gambling dependency. These include:

- It requires the caller to take the first step.
- Control remains with the caller.
- The caller can remain completely anonymous.
- It can provide a service that is low cost to the caller.
- It is readily available.
- It doesn't involve travelling or appointments.
- The conversation can be taken on trust.
- It can be a means of instant relief.
- The helpline can develop into an effective counselling medium.

Receiving Calls

When operating a helpline for a gambling dependency it is important that the recipient of the call acts professionally. This is enhanced by:

- Being open.

- Listening actively.
- Checking caller motivation.
- Encouraging change.
- Reinforcing positives.
- Suggesting self-help strategies.
- Providing good-quality information.
- Guiding the conversation towards a safe ending.

9   A Structure for Effective Intervention

I feel stronger now that counselling has sorted out the turmoil. My life is so much better since I got rid of the gambling nightmare. I have a greater understanding of who I am and how I react.

(City trader, aged 30)

There are a number of different ways to provide effective intervention to help the problem gambler. These range from simply befriending the person with the dependency to long-term psychotherapy to explore in depth unconscious reasons and motivations lying behind the addiction. What is appropriate will depend on the age, personality and circumstances of the individual, the reason why the gambler wishes to address their dependency, and the availability of treatment. What is effective may also depend on these factors but is likely to be reliant on the continuity of the scheduled course of treatment, the ability and willingness of the gambler to change their behaviour and the skill of the person working with them.

Range of Approaches

The truth of the matter in the UK is that there remains a shortage of facilities where someone affected by a gambling dependency can seek help. Unlike a drug or alcohol dependency where there are a range of services that offer treatment, until very recently services for gamblers have been fragmented and ad hoc. There are a small number of specialist facilities but most have started up in piecemeal fashion either because the clientele of an agency have presented with the problem or because staff employed by an agency have a particular interest. Likewise, the methods of intervention have developed in individual fashion. Within my knowledge they can be categorised in general terms, as follows:

The community agency approach. In this category I would include the type of approach adopted by probation officers, prison staff, social workers, advice centre personnel, youth workers, and similar agencies. The role of the worker is often one that is partly 'befriender', partly that of a control agent, and partly that of adviser/counsellor. This sort of approach is likely to focus on encouraging motivation and behaviour adaptation.

The self-help response. This could range from an individual who is able, with help from friends or family, to break the dependency without recourse to an outside agency to the nation-wide self-help organisation Gamblers Anonymous (see Chapter 10). This type of approach is heavily reliant on providing support and an empathic understanding and can sustain them through a prolonged period of abstinence that enables the adoption of a changed lifestyle.

Residential facilities. The only dedicated residential facility for problem gamblers in the UK is that of the Gordon House Association (see Chapter 11) which combines elements of self-help with that of in-depth counselling. Commercial organisations such as Promis or the Charter Clinic (see Chapter15) offer a residential service based on individual and group counselling for problem gamblers who are able to afford the substantial fees. A small number of religious communities also suggest that gambling is included among the problem areas with which they can help.

Counselling agencies and individuals. After Gamblers Anonymous the widest provision is undoubtedly that covered by counselling agencies. Whilst there is not yet a broad and comprehensive network of such services the task is being undertaken by GamCare (see Chapter 14). A number of agencies around the UK supplemented by the work of a few individuals provide a facility for those affected by a gambling dependency (see Chapter 15). The style of working varies but for many the emphasis is on motivational interviewing and/or a cognitive/behavioural approach. It is interesting to note that the majority of these agencies have grown up in the voluntary sector. I know of only two that operate within a National Health Service (NHS) Trust scheme.

Towards Effective Intervention

Whatever the approach to working with someone affected by a gambling dependency there is a foundation of factors that will enhance the opportunity for effective intervention. The following list is an adaptation of material drawn from *Working with Young Problem Gamblers: Guidelines to Practice* (Bellringer 1993).

Understand the Issues

Before attempting to work with a problem gambler it is essential to understand gambling in the context of today's society and its place within the culture of groups of people. The issues concern both positive and negative aspects of gambling and what is attractive to which age groups. Some of the principal aspects to consider and questions to ask are:

- *The range of gambling activities in the UK.* What can you gamble on legally? Are there illegal gaming activities operating locally and is that likely to attract problem gamblers?

- *Availability of gambling.* What are the age and other restrictions that apply to various gambling activities (a confused picture in this country)? Where can you just walk in and where do you have to wait before you can gamble? Are they applied rigorously or is the law flouted? What voluntary or trade-imposed age restrictions apply?

- *The location of gambling.* What gambling activities are available in the area of the problem gambler? Which are available directly from home, such as telephone betting or the Internet? What can be found by walking down the High Street? What else is available elsewhere?

- *Gambling and its place in society.* What is the role of gambling in today's society? How is it perceived by the public, by government and by the gaming industry? What are the benefits and drawbacks to legitimising a wide range of gambling in society?

- *The acceptability of gambling.* Does everyone accept it? What are the legal and moral issues? Why is it acceptable? Who gains and who loses? Why is it so attractive? Are there groups of people who are more attracted to gambling than others?

- *Gambling and revenue.* Is it right to tax gambling? What are the arguments for using gambling products to raise money for charities and 'good causes'? How much money does the government collect from gambling and what happens to it?

- *The gaming industry.* What contribution does the gaming industry make to society? Should they be doing more? Should they help pay for the problems associated with gambling? What is their response to problem gambling? How do they respond if approached about a gambler's problem?

- *Responsibility and gambling.* Are all forms of gambling relatively harmless or are some less so than others? Do we need tight regulation on gambling or are we interfering in the rights of an individual by doing so? Is it right to treat the growth of gambling with caution? Should young people be protected from gambling? Are they now?

- *Gambling as a problem.* To what extent does gambling cause problems? Is problem gambling simply the fault of individuals who are weak? How many are affected by a gambling dependency? Why can't they just stop?

- *Danger signs and symptoms.* How easy is it to spot the problem gambler? What are the signs to look for? Do different problem gamblers display different symptoms?

- *Vulnerability.* Are some people more vulnerable than others? What are the predisposing factors that may lead to a gambling dependency? What drives a social gambler to cross the line into problem gambling?

- *Help available.* Is problem gambling an issue that you or your agency are equipped to deal with confidently and effectively? What other help is available in your area? Are different types of help likely to be more suitable for some problem gamblers than others?

A Structure for Change

Whatever the approach to someone who is seeking help in addressing their gambling dependency a principal objective has to be encouraging them to change their behaviour. Having a clear structure for the change process is, for the majority of approaches, a necessary first step. It is useful to adapt a method of changing behaviour that you have used effectively with other problems or develop one that you consider to be suitable. Whichever method you choose, it must be with the full agreement of the person affected by a gambling dependency. It must be easily understood, and one with which you both feel comfortable.

The following is a change structure that in my experience works well in the context of problem gambling. It is easy to follow and progress through the stages can be readily identified. It is imperative to involve the problem gambler fully throughout the process and check regularly with other people directly affected. Agreed boundaries of confidentiality must, however, be preserved at all times.

First Phase: Assessment and Diagnosis

Identify the problem

- Check whether there is a real gambling problem. This may be achieved in a focused conversation with the gambler or by using an assessment checklist (see later). The extent to which it is causing difficulties should help shape the treatment approach.

- Check whose problem it is. The gambler may be reluctant to see that the problem is theirs or may be gambling excessively as a reaction to another's behaviour. For instance, a teenager may be gambling as a rebellion against parents and their value system.

- Check that the problem gambler wants to change and to what extent. Even when gamblers recognise it is a problem for them they may perceive significant change, such as giving up gambling altogether, as too difficult or unnecessary. For example, I recall a female who had a problem playing machines in her local bingo club. Whilst she wanted help to stop playing the machines she did not want to give up the social benefits of playing bingo with her friends.

Consider change

- It needs to be kept in mind that change is a difficult and complex process. For the gambler who has spent years avoiding change and running away from painful situations it can appear particularly daunting. The skill is in encouraging and exploring with the gambler that it is something *they* want.

- Even a small degree of change in lifestyle or behaviour can be construed as a considerable achievement and can be the catalyst for more significant movement. For example, I remember a problem gambler who, for the first time in years, managed to curtail his gambling so as to have sufficient money left to buy a birthday present for his daughter. This led to a rapprochement with his family which in turn provided the impetus to break his gambling dependency.

- Gamblers may want instant change and set themselves an impossible target. It is well to keep in mind that each step towards change must be attainable and that this incremental approach is more likely to lead to lifetime behaviour modification.

Identify objectives

- Both the counsellor and the gambler need to be clear about what can realistically be achieved in the time-scale of the treatment sessions. An initial number of sessions needs to be established with the last being that of reflection and review. If the treatment approach is one where the direction comes from the gambler it is useful to get them to focus on what they want to achieve. If the direction is more shared, for example in a probation officer–offender supervisory situation, the identification and agreement about objectives becomes more of a joint exercise.

- Consider situations that should be avoided. Bearing in mind that problem gamblers are vulnerable towards developing a dependency, little positive change would be achieved if they went from heavy gambling to heavy drinking. During this assessment phase the possibility of multiple dependency involving alcohol, drugs or other psychological addictions should be explored.

- Although I would advocate that someone with a gambling problem should, whilst breaking the dependency, totally abstain from gambling, the prospect of doing so may be too daunting for some. It is therefore important to agree at the outset whether, during the sessions, the objective is abstinence or controlled gambling.

Measure objectives

- It is also important to be clear on how the objectives are to be measured. Bearing in mind that a problem gambler is usually an expert at lying and being 'economic with the truth' it is valuable to cover this aspect during the assessment process. Even if measuring of objectives is reliant on self-reporting this process can be enhanced by a written record being kept. Commonly, one agreed objective is likely to be the cessation of all gambling. The most simple record is that of ticking a calendar each day they do not gamble. Keeping a daily diary or journal that charts how that objective is achieved provides a more comprehensive record that may be useful in future work with the gambler.

Explore causes

Whilst the exploration of causes should take place within this initial phase the feelings and experiences of the gambler should be revisited and checked throughout the counselling process.

- A look at the background and early experiences of the gambler enables both the counsellor and the problem gambler to reflect on how these may have contributed to the dependency. Take, for example, an ex-public schoolboy who perceives his parents' insistence that he went to boarding school as a demonstration of their lack of love for him. Checking out his feelings then and now, how he reacted to the situation and how that related to the onset of his gambling career, is likely, when considered with other background factors, to provide some insight as to why gambling became overly important.

- Information about the family, the gambler's role and position within it, their value systems and the family attitude towards gambling will help create an overall picture and give further possible clues as to why the person turned to gambling. It may be that at the start of counselling the gambler articulates an idealised family but later on is able to face the pain of disclosing a very different picture. It is, therefore, worth revisiting background experiences throughout the counselling period.

- The present circumstances of the gambler are also worth exploring in some depth. They may be reinforcing earlier negative experiences or they may throw up possible reasons why the gambler seeks solace with a machine, at the betting office or in a casino. The more the gambler can be encouraged to talk about their life and their response to it, the greater the opportunity to reflect this back and develop insight.

- Of equal importance is the need to explore the driving force that pitched the individual from social to problem gambling. In many cases the gambler may not know and the likely reasons do not appear to be clear. Background history should, of course, provide strong clues as to whether they have principally been drawn to gambling in order to escape from pressures and problems, as an act of rebellion against other people, as a means of feeling empowered and in control, or for the excitement and thrill of the action. A careful look at these 'drivers' can then be used to help shape the options that the gambler wants to consider to change their behaviour.

Second Phase: Design

Consider options

- Having explored with the gambler their background experiences, and their current situation and how gambling appears to be meeting their needs, the focus should shift back to the objectives that the individual would like to achieve. At this point in the process I would suggest it is helpful to encourage the gambler to think about a wide range of possible options for each identified objective. The realistic possibility of achieving these can be left until later as the value of generating ideas may be diminished if they are discarded on pragmatic grounds too early in the process.

- It is, however, useful to explore with them possible ways that the favoured options could be achieved – what it would take from the individual and from others, how long it would take to achieve, how it might lead on to other possibilities, and so on.

Assess options

- Having spent time exploring a range of options, each one needs to be assessed. This may be carried out simply in a two-way conversation with the counsellor encouraging and prompting the gambler to formulate an opinion. More imaginative assessment methods can also be used. Diagrams, charts, research findings, and checklists of pros and cons are examples of how the gambler can be encouraged to become involved in the process. This exercise in itself is likely to give a positive boost to their self-esteem and additionally gives them an immediate interest to occupy the time previously spent gambling.

- Against each option the gambler should be encouraged to assess how realistic the option is; likely gains or losses to their quality of life; what are the costs and benefits materially, financially and emotionally; the extent to which it will achieve the particular objective to which it relates; and its likely contribution to permanently breaking the gambling dependency.

Third phase: Action

Agree options

Once the options have been explored and assessed against their objectives the gambler should be encouraged to decide which of them they wish to pursue. It is useful at this stage to introduce a time framework and to prioritise both objectives and options within that. Take, as an example, an objective to create a better life for their family – an option to achieving that is to buy a house. The time-scale of achieving that would depend on factors such as whether there were significant debts to pay off, whether there was any capital that could be realised, and the employment status of the gambler.

Plan action

- Planning may or may not be a skill that the gambler perceives they possess but it may be useful to remind them that obtaining the money that they needed to gamble almost certainly required careful planning.

- The gambler should be encouraged to consult with everyone who will be involved in carrying through the option. This in itself may raise the gambler's anxiety as they are likely to have withdrawn into their own secretive world. On the other hand in doing so it is probable that they will find others involved to be both helpful and supportive.

- Encourage the gambler to think about a strategy for carrying through the option and to put it within a time-scale. When looking at time-scales it is useful to suggest an element of flexibility so as to avoid feelings of failure if, for whatever reason, there are delays in carrying through the option.

- Help the gambler come to a decision on what method of change they feel is achievable and that with which they feel comfortable. Some will favour an incremental approach to change while others may opt for the 'big bang' – immediate total change. Whichever it is, it will be useful to explore the possibility of failure and how to cope with it.

Carry through

- Responsibility for any change must, of course, remain with the gambler. When they were gambling out of control they would have consistently tried to shift responsibility away from themselves. We have already established that an essential first step to breaking a gambling dependency is for the gambler to accept responsibility for their own actions. Similarly, they need to be able to own the change.

- Avoid assumptions by discussing every situation with the gambler and any other people encompassed in the counselling. Positive encouragement as the gambler begins to put their plans into action is likely to do much to help them sustain the effort.

- It is useful to remember, and to remind the gambler, that the more ambitious the change, the greater the risk of failure. Be ready for a lapse back into gambling or depression associated with failing to achieve an element of change. Use time to explore the reasons and as a positive learning exercise.

Assessment Interviews

Before addressing the gambling dependency it is important to establish the extent of the problem. Commonly, this is done by using a method of assessment. There are a number of these used, some of which have been adapted from those designed for assessing other dependencies. The following assessment checklist used by GamCare has been devised from my own experience combined with an adaptation of the Gambler's Anonymous list of questions (Gamblers Anonymous 1997) and DSM-IV (Diagnostic and Statistical Manual) criteria for pathological gambling (Lesieur and Rosenthal 1991). I would suggest that scoring several afirmative answers to this set of questions will provide a good indication as to the severity of the gambling problem. If only a few questions are answered positively it gives an indication that gambling is becoming a serious problem.

- Have you become more and more preoccupied with gambling by reliving experiences, studying systems, planning gambling sessions or obtaining money to gamble?

- When you win do you have a strong desire to continue gambling?

- Do you need to gamble with more and more money in order to satisfy a need for excitement?

- Do you 'chase losses' by continuing or quickly returning to gamble when on a losing streak?

- Do you gamble for long periods and do so longer than planned?

- Do you gamble as a means of escaping from problems or other intolerable feelings?

- Do you try to hide the extent of your gambling?

- Do you manipulate situations in order to give you an excuse to gamble?

- Have you put at risk important or significant relationships, educational studies, a job or your career because of gambling?

- Do you become restless, irritable or moody when you cannot gamble or when you have attempted to cut down or stop gambling?

- Are you reluctant to spend 'gambling money' on anything else?

- When not actually gambling do you spend time obtaining or planning how to raise money to gamble again?

- Do you ever gamble until you have no money left?

- Are you in debt because of gambling?

- Do you gamble to get money to pay debts or to solve financial problems?

- Do you lie to get money for gambling or to pay off gambling debts?

- Have you ever 'borrowed' without prior permission in order to pay off debts or to get money to gamble?

- Have you ever sold your own, your family's or other people's possessions to get money to gamble or to pay off gambling debts?

- Have you ever had to ask another person for money in order to pay off a pressing debt created by gambling?

- Have you ever committed illegal acts such as theft, forgery or fraud in order to finance your gambling?

Issues to Consider

There are a number of issues that have a bearing on the effectiveness of intervention and the following are those that I consider to be of particular importance.

Confidentiality

It is vital from the outset to reach a clear understanding with the problem gambler regarding confidentiality. The extent to which information can be shared with family members, friends, or agency personnel must be fully discussed and agreed by everyone concerned.

Short- or Long-term Involvement

The length of time that should be spent addressing a gambling dependency will depend on several factors. Two of the most important are likely to be the constraints of the agency and the ability of the gambler to sustain their commitment.

On a one-to-one basis is it common to limit each session to a maximum of an hour, as anything beyond this is likely to become increasingly difficult for concentration to be sustained by both the problem gambler and the counsellor. In a group setting the time can, of course, be extended but intensive focused work should also be limited.

The number of sessions relates to the counselling approach used, but in my experience initial work with a problem gambler is effective with an assessment interview followed by between four and six further sessions. At this point progress can be reviewed and the need for a further batch of sessions explored.

It is a matter of some controversy as to which is the most effective way to work with problem gamblers, and in my view there is no one, best way. However, I am firmly of the opinion that when the focus of the intervention is that of the affect of the gambling dependency, short-term problem-centred counselling works well. The primary aim is to encourage them to share how they have responded to past experiences, relating that to the 'here and now', and exploring with them how they might adapt their responses to achieve more positive outcomes. There are a number of approaches that suit this type of intervention. My own experience of working with, or being involved in, counselling processes that have addressed an individual's gambling dependency have tended to include the following:

- **Motivational interviewing** whereby the counsellor seeks to determine the level of the gambler's motivation, emphasises positive factors, and encourages the gambler to set and achieve attainable goals that enable them to take charge of their own life again.

- **Cognitive behaviour** whereby the counsellor explores with the gambler their experiences, how they interpret their experiences and how they consequently structure their own approach to life. The key is to encourage and assist them to change their thinking process to enable them to then effectively change their behaviour.

- **Transactional analysis** which provides a framework that aids the gambler in understanding how they respond to situations and interactions with other people. It can then be used as a learning tool that helps the gambler adapt more appropriate responses.

When, during the course of this short-term intervention, it becomes clear that other serious issues need to be addressed (for example, clinical depression), and the gambler is in agreement, longer-term psychoanalytic counselling may be appropriate.

Building Self-esteem

The problem gambler's level of self-esteem will almost certainly be low. The restoration of confidence and the restructuring of self-esteem will require careful and sensitive handling. The gambler therefore needs to be valued as an individual and be given both the responsibility and authority to make their own decisions. If adopting a structure for change like the one outlined above, it is important to agree short-term goals that are achievable and put in a time-scale that is comfortable for the gambler. When they are achieved or the time-scale comes to an end, review them. If the gambler wishes to go further, encourage revision and, when appropriate, consider medium- and long-term goals. Factors that are likely to contribute to building self-esteem include:

- Take an encouraging stance at all times.

- Turn negatives into positives whenever possible. For example turn a lapse back to gambling from being seen by the gambler as a failure to emphasise it was preceded by success and can be used as a learning experience.

- Chart progress with graphs, tables, lists and other techniques to make progress visually easy.

- Enable and encourage the gambler to feel a sense of achievement.

- Use the 'one day at a time' principle which will usually tie in with the problem gambler's 'here and now' attitude.

- If you need to be critical, limit negatives to an absolute minimum; always do so in a constructive fashion, balance with positives, and check carefully as to whether the problem gambler accepts and agrees with any criticism.

- Reward success with praise, relaxing of any controls, and by other appropriate methods. Suggest that problem gamblers reward themselves by, for instance, spending some of the money saved by not gambling on something personal.

- Constantly encourage involvement in a range of activities in which the problem gambler possesses some skills or has expressed an interest.

- End each session on a positive note.

Age

The age of the gambler and the length of time that gambling has been a problem are both important factors to consider. For the young problem gambler who has been dependent on gambling for a year or two during the transition through adolescence it can be seen as a phase in their life. In my experience many young gamblers are able to break the dependency relatively quickly and move on, either through their own efforts or with the help of a counsellor.

For the older gambler who has been into heavy gambling over a number of years the likelihood is that it has become an ingrained lifestyle. In these cases the dependency may be much harder to overcome. It is one reason why older gamblers are more likely to gamble until they experience a devastating self-destructive 'rock bottom'. It is only the humiliation of this that dredges up sufficient motivation to look seriously at changing their behaviour.

Incidentally, I would suggest that as a rough guide this split is also useful in advocating a return to controlled gambling or lifetime abstinence. For a teenager it is of little use to say that you must not gamble for the rest of your life. At that age it has no meaning as the young person is unlikely to have planned 'the rest of their life'. Additionally, when the dependency has been successfully overcome and is linked to a short-term phase in their life, it is unlikely that further gambling will have the same effect. For the older, long-term gambler, it may be a very different matter. Even when the dependency has been overcome it may be wise to avoid all gambling in the future, and certainly the harder forms of gambling.

Family Involvement

We have already established that the motivation to change is often precipitated by the threat of family break-up (see Chapter 7). The family can also play a key role in assisting the process of change. This can be very direct as, for instance, when it is appropriate to undertake couple counselling. One or more family members playing a supportive role can make all the difference to the problem gambler managing to sustain change. This can work in two ways: it can make gamblers feel loved and valued despite what they have done or, when their self-esteem is so low and they are unable to accept changing for their own good, they can do it for the benefit of someone else.

Transferring Dependency

A great danger for anyone vulnerable to problem gambling is that they will transfer the dependency to something else. It is therefore helpful to bring this possibility into the counselling session and explore ways of avoiding the danger. The desirable state is one where the individual is reliant on a wide portfolio of interests and people.

Group Work with Problem Gamblers

The structure for change and the factors to take into consideration equally apply should you be running a group to address a gambling dependency. Helpful strategies in this approach are likely to include the following:

Involving group members in setting ground rules. This is a very effective means of gaining ownership from the start and of avoiding arguments and discussions that detract from the group's objective.

Establishing at the beginning what is meant by the term 'confidential'. This is crucially important. It would be important to state that what is said within the group remains confidential to it, but this has to be done in the context of corporate responsibility of the agency and any statutory requirement to pass on disclosure of serious criminality – a distinct possibility in a group of problem gamblers. A discussion on confidentiality would also cover note-taking or other means of recording group sessions used by the facilitator and the purpose for doing so.

An underlying theme of positive behaviour modification. This should be a central group norm and members of the group should be asked to subscribe to this concept and to practise it at all times when they are participating in the group process.

The adoption of a non-judgemental style. This is a further important element in encouraging ownership of the group by all its members.

This needs to be clearly stated at the beginning of the group process and members periodically reminded of it, particularly when one or more members has experienced a gambling relapse between group sessions. It can prove very beneficial in encouraging an enabling ethos among the whole group.

Writing a fun element into the group content. This can help in a number of ways: it makes attendance and participation a more pleasurable experience; it provides a safety valve that can help defuse a tense situation; and it provides some lighter moments to counter the inevitably heavy and painful aspects the gamblers may recount.

The inclusion of imaginative and innovative content. Part of this input should ideally have been contributed by group members themselves. In my experience, role play, for instance, offers a wide range of opportunities but should only be undertaken by experienced facilitators that can keep control of this powerful learning tool and can successfully de-role participants at the end of the session.

A flexible and adaptable approach to the group. This needs to take account of the disparate personalities involved and accommodate change necessitated by an important disclosure that needs to be further explored.

Encouraging the sharing of experience. This may seem an obvious aspect to include but for someone with a gambling dependency it can be particularly rewarding. Most problem gamblers are able to remember their experiences and the pain associated with them, and when shared can provide a key for other group members to make sense of what they have felt. It can also help group members collaborate on the formulation of relapse prevention strategies.

Activities written into the group programme. Depending on the nature of the group and available resources, these may take place away from the usual venue as well as within it. Those activities that might reinforce a need to adapt would be particularly useful.

Extensive use of diaries, charts, graphs and so on. These are helpful for the individual member and for the group as a whole. Because of the nature of problem gamblers, care needs to be taken to ensure nobody is left feeling scapegoated or belittled when comparisons are highlighted. On the other hand, a positive competitiveness can be a useful encouragement for those who seek to improve on what they have achieved.

Facilitating alternative activities to gambling. This is possibly an easier prospect for an agency than it is for the individual. Having been given the lead and, if appropriate, financial support, the group members should be encouraged to find out what is on offer and to organise their involvement in the activity. Clearly, this will help to fill the void created once they have stopped gambling. The taking part in activities together should also help socialisation between members and enable them to relearn the skills needed to get on with people and to develop human relationships.

Individual contact. Each group member should be afforded this to enable personal difficulties to be aired and, if necessary, adaptations to be made to the programme. It also provides an opportunity to check out individual progress which might differ from what has been claimed in the group setting.

Evaluation. The group process and progress made by members of the group need to be evaluated. Involvement of the group in any assessment is a useful method of feedback and can help reinforce positives. From what has been said earlier in the book, nurturing self-esteem is particularly valuable in encouraging change in a problem gambler, and a good group experience can do much towards achieving this goal.

SUMMARY

There are a number of ways in which a problem gambler might be effectively helped to break their dependency. These can be broadly divided into approaches provided though a community agency such as the probation service, self-help groups epitomised by GA, residential facilities such as Gordon House, and counselling sessions available through individuals or organisations like GamCare. As a principal objective of effective intervention is to encourage change, having a clear structure for the change process is an important first step. Assessment of the extent of the problem and careful consideration of factors that might influence the change process are essential whether working with an individual problem gambler or with a group.

CHECKLIST

Having a structure for change is likely to help the problem gambler understand and work through the process. Figure 9.1 is a representatiion in diagrammatic form of the example detailed earlier (Bellringer 1993):

Phase 1		Phase 2		Phase 3
DIAGNOSIS	⇑⇒	**DESIGN**	⇑⇒	**ACTION**
⇓	⇑	⇓	⇑	⇓
Identify problem	⇑	⇓	⇑	⇓
⇓	⇑	⇓	⇑	Agree options
Consider change	⇑	Consider options	⇑	⇓
⇓	⇑	⇓	⇑	⇓
Decide objectives	⇑	⇓	⇑	Plan action
⇓	⇑	Assess options	⇑	⇓
Measure objectives	⇑	⇓	⇑	⇓
⇓	⇑	⇓	⇑	Carry through
⇒⇒⇒⇒⇒⇒⇒	⇑	⇒⇒⇒⇒⇒⇒⇒	⇑	⇓

Figure 9.1 Three-phase Structure for Change

Issues to Consider

Important issues that will have a bearing on effective intervention with an individual problem gambler are likely to include:

- Confidentiality.

- The length of involvement.

- Building self-esteem.

- The age of the gambler.

- Family involvement.

- Dependency transference.

In addition to the above, strategies that are likely to be helpful when undertaking group work with problem gamblers might include:

- Involving the group in setting ground rules.

- Establishing at the start what the term 'confidential' means.

- The underlying theme being that of positive behaviour modification.

- Adopting a non-judgemental style.

- Writing a fun element into group content.

- Including imaginative and innovative content.

- Adopting a flexible and adaptable approach.
- Encouraging the sharing of experience.
- Activities within the group programme.
- The use of diaries, charts, graphs and other visual records.

10 Self-help Groups

It works because you are talking to yourself.

(Mick – GA member)

This chapter looks at the contribution made in assisting those affected by a gambling dependency by the self-help group. I am aware that a number of such groups are operating in the UK either through the efforts of individuals or with the support and encouragement of agencies. These are mostly small-scale and usually function as part of a wider service provided by a religious group or counselling agency. A larger, internationally active and well known self-help group is that of the fellowship of Gamblers Anonymous (GA) and its sister organisation, Gam-Anon. It is therefore these that will be the focus of this chapter.

How Did Gamblers Anonymous Begin?

The following explanation has been adapted from *Questions and Answers about the Problem of Compulsive Gambling and the GA Recovery Programme*. GA started from a chance meeting between two gamblers who had experienced severe problems. They started to meet on a regular basis and through mutual support managed to abstain from gambling. They concluded that in order to prevent any return to gambling they needed to bring about some behavioural changes within themselves. They adopted a model of spiritual principles that were already being used by people with other addictive behaviours. Wanting to carry the message of hope to other problem gamblers, they went public. Favourable publicity led to the first meeting of Gamblers Anonymous which took place in Los Angeles in September 1957.

The first GA group in the UK was established in Belfast in 1962. A short while later the Reverend Gordon Moody, a Methodist minister from England, was approached by an American and his wife after he had addressed a church meeting on the subject of gambling. The visitor was a member of a GA group in Brooklyn, New York, and he inspired Gordon Moody to found the first English meeting in 1964.

What Is Gamblers Anonymous?

This may best be answered by quoting the 'Preamble to a Gamblers Anonymous Meeting' (*New Life* 1998, p. 3):

> Gamblers Anonymous is a fellowship of men and women who share their experience, strength and hope with each other that they may solve their gambling problem and help others to do the same. The only requirement for membership is a desire to stop gambling. There are no dues or fees for GA membership; it is self-supporting through its own voluntary contributions. GA is not allied with any sect, denomination, politics, organisation or institution; does not wish to engage in any controversy; and neither endorses nor opposes any causes. Its primary purpose is to stop gambling and help other compulsive gamblers to do the same.

Taking the UK and Eire together, there are around 200 meetings held each week to which anyone with a gambling problem can just turn up. There is a branch secretary and the meeting is chaired by any member. The core of the meeting is to offer support and understanding to fellow sufferers of compulsive gambling. Newcomers are invited to 'give a therapy' whereby they describe their gambling history and what it has done to them and to others. More established members will often update the meeting on their progress to overcome the compulsion and will offer words of encouragement and advice to new members of the group and to those who have lapsed or are feeling under pressure.

All speakers begin in the same way, so if I was at a meeting I would begin with:

My name is Paul and I am a compulsive gambler.

Gamblers Anonymous has its own helpline that is staffed by members of GA and Gam-Anon. Callers are encouraged to attend a meeting. Outside the meeting further support may be offered in dealing with crises such as managing debt or setting up regular contact for those whose resolve to abstain from gambling is under pressure.

GA expects its members to abstain from all forms of gambling for the rest of their lives. A failure to achieve this does not exclude gamblers from membership but at the weekly meetings they are likely to be pressurised to keep trying. Those who are suspected of lying or covering up about their gambling are likely to be questioned by fellow members. However, the programme is based on personal acceptance of the need to stop gambling and many members have a long association with GA before they manage to give up gambling entirely.

As there are no statutory dues or fees to pay for membership and the fellowship does not accept outside contributions, GA relies on voluntary donations from its members for necessary financial support.

Having had a professional link with Gamblers Anonymous over a number of years I am aware that whilst the fellowship is not divided by age, gender or ethnicity, some community groups have been less well represented than others. For example, it is known that gambling is very much part of the Chinese culture yet, anecdotally, few problem gamblers from this community are seen at GA or, for that matter, at other helping agencies. I know of some young problem gamblers who have gained real benefit from attending GA and of others who have found little commonality between their lifestyle and that of the majority of older members. I have also been told that women can feel uncomfortable when they find themselves in a minority of one at a meeting or when they are identified with the predominantly female Gam-Anon group. On the other hand, and despite the uncomfortable feelings, female problem gamblers have derived great strength from attending regular meetings.

Whilst a GA group meeting will never be able to provide the answer for every problem gambler, there is no doubt that thousands of people across the world have found that the fellowship of GA and its particular recovery programme works for them.

The Twelve-step Recovery Programme

At the core of the GA approach is the twelve-step recovery programme. This 'life plan', conceived in the 1930s, is believed to have first been used in the US to address alcohol addiction. It was a natural step for those grappling with a gambling problem to use the model already established by those trying to overcome an alcohol dependency. Nowadays it is also used as the central structure of, or as an addition to, a range of dependency recovery programmes.

Wide international acceptance of this programme is perhaps an indication of its perceived effectiveness. Whilst several of the steps refer to 'a higher power' and to God, the fellowship of GA stresses that this should always be interpreted as 'the God of your own understanding'.

The following is an explanation of how the twelve steps divide into three sections, and it provides a useful description as to how the programme works. It was written by 'Peter', a recovering problem gambler, for *GamCare News* (1998, p. 6). It is followed by an abbreviated explanation of the steps taken from 'The Twelve Steps of Recovery' (Gambler's Anonymous 1994). I have added a few comments after each step in an endeavour to highlight aspects that appear to me to have a resonance with other approaches.

> To a normal person the twelve-step programme of recovery may appear very confusing, but it can be divided into three parts:
>
> **Acceptance** (steps one to three) that 'being addicted' meant being out of control, and that being out of control meant being unable to solve my addiction alone.
>
> **Repair** (steps four to nine) is the continuous process of healing myself and my relationships with others, and so distancing myself from my addiction.
>
> **Memory** (steps ten to twelve) is never forgetting that the addiction is dormant and not eliminated. Regular attendance at GA meetings serves as a reminder of what I used to do and how I used to behave. Without this help I would become complacent and could easily slip back into addictive behaviour, even picking up a different addiction.
>
> The programme has nothing to do with gambling, but everything to do with recovery from addictive behaviour through shared self-help.

> **Step One: We admitted we were powerless over gambling – that our lives had become unmanageable.** We come to believe that only through utter defeat are we able to take our first steps towards sanity and strength. Our admission of personal defeat turns out to be our foundation upon which happy and purposeful lives may be built.

This is a sound beginning – recognition that the gambling addiction has taken over your life and that you have to change significantly.

> **Step Two: Came to believe that a Power greater than ourselves could restore us to a normal way of thinking and living.** Defiance and lying are the outstanding characteristics of many gamblers, so it is not uncommon that many of us have had days of defying God. True humility and an open mind can lead us to a Power greater than ourselves and will, in time, take us to God, love of man, and a normal way of life.

This combination of humility and an open mind can, when handled sensitively so as not to damage the fragile self-esteem of the gambler, create a foundation for rebuilding a lifestyle that is not reliant on gambling.

Step Three: Made a decision to turn our will and our lives over to the care of this Power of our own understanding. The first two steps asked you to believe and accept. Step three calls for willingness to do something, and to turn away from self-will.

The willingness to take action and overcome the fear of leaving the comfort of the familiar pattern of your life is an important step.

Step Four: Made a searching and fearless moral and financial inventory of ourselves. We have gambled to get away from responsibility, fears, frustrations and depressions. We have envisioned great dreams of wealth and position when we would repay those we harmed by gambling. In GA, we slowly learn that something has to be done about our vengeful resentments, self-pity and unwarranted pride. Our financial problem must be examined.

This self-examination is of great value to the recovering problem gambler and is a key element in maintaining a gambling-free lifestyle. Over the years I have come across a number of long-term members of GA who display a greater honesty in their approach to life than the majority of people appear to do.

Step Five: Admitted to ourselves and another human being the exact nature of our wrong. This step will deflate your ego. If we want to get rid of yesterday's guilt and torments, we must talk with someone about them. This step is the means of learning the art of forgiveness. This feeling of being one with God and man, through the open and honest sharing of our terrible sense of guilt, brings us rest and peace of mind where we may prepare ourselves for the following steps towards a full and meaningful life – free of gambling.

In my view this step has a value beyond purging guilt through the confessional. Talking about gambling with an active listener provides an element of insight as to what led to the dependency. It then enables gamblers to reconstruct their lives with a greater awareness of what 'drives' them and can, hopefully, enable them to avoid reacting in the same way as they have in the past.

Step Six: We were entirely ready to have these defects of character removed. Through step six we establish a willingness to become mature men and women, sincerely trying to grow. Perfection is a goal we may strive for, but never quite reach; however, it is urgent that we make a beginning and keep trying. The moment we say 'No', our minds close against the grace of God.

This naturally follows from Step Five. Having admitted and begun to understand the problems caused by your previous approach, constructing a set of responses that is beneficial to you, your family and friends and the community at large takes the individual towards greater maturity. This in turn begins to meet some of the personal needs that previously motivated the gambler's dependency.

Step Seven: Humbly asked God (of our understanding) to remove our shortcomings. When we have taken a square look at some of our defects, discussed them with another, and have become willing to have them removed, our thinking about humility commences to have a wider meaning. We enjoy moments in which there is something like real peace of mind. To those of us who have hitherto known only excitement, depression or anxiety this new-found peace is a priceless gift.

The new-found peace that is gained from stepping off the treadmill of a gambling addiction is a valuable realisation to the recovering problem gambler. It can provide the spur to continue and the means of resisting a return to gambling. Humbly accepting that the pursuit of the previous lifestyle brought pain to the individual and to others can assist in the process of feeling good about change.

Step Eight: Made a list of all persons we had harmed and became willing to make amends to them all. This step is concerned with personal relations. We must first take a look backwards and try and discover where we were at fault. Next, we make an honest attempt to repair the damage we have done. With our new-found knowledge of ourselves, we may develop the best possible relations with every human being we know.

Certainly, looking at the harm caused has value, and re-establishing good relations is important for the self-confidence of the gambler and for the understanding of the victim. It is also important for the gambler to understand why their behaviour was so destructive and how that period is likely to affect current and future relationships.

Step Nine: Made direct amends to such people whenever possible, except when to do so would injure them or others. First, we will wish to be reasonably certain that we are making the GA programme. Then we are ready to go to these people, telling them what GA is and what we are trying to do. With this background we can freely admit the damage we have done and make our apologies. We can pay or promise to pay whatever obligations, financial or otherwise, we owe.

The value of this step is that when the apologies are accepted and people respond positively to the gamblers' efforts to change it boosts their confidence and gives them an incentive to continue. Many consider themselves to be unloved and unlovable. The realisation that this was part myth and part skewed thinking is a powerful motivation to conquer the dependency. This includes the act of financially paying back money 'borrowed' or stolen and repaying debts. Whilst it might be a long process it can give the recovering problem gambler a real sense of achievement and purge some of the guilt.

Step Ten: Continued to take personal inventory and when we were wrong, promptly admitted it. With step ten we begin to put our GA way of living to practical use, day by day. Our inventory enables us to settle with the past. We are really able to leave it behind us. We need to develop a willingness to admit when the fault is ours and an equal willingness to forgive when the fault is elsewhere. The development of self-restraint; ceasing to make unreasonable demands on those we love; courtesy, kindness, justice and love are keynotes by which we may come into harmony with practically anyone. An honest regret for harms done, a genuine gratitude for blessing received, and a willingness to try for better things tomorrow are the permanent assets we should seek.

This code of conduct is to be admired and I have met a number of GA members who appear to live up to it. It is, however, an aspiration – an ideal state and something to strive towards.

Step Eleven: Sought through prayer and meditation to improve our conscious contact with God as we understand Him, praying only for knowledge of His will for us and the power to carry that out. As we have seen, self-searching is the means by which we bring new vision, action and grace to bear upon the dark and negative side of our natures. It is a step in the development of the kind of humility that makes it possible for us to receive God's help.

The reflectiveness of this step is important – It is a memory step described above, it reminds people of the need not to lose sight of where their gambling has taken them and the advantages of permanently breaking the dependency.

> **Step Twelve: Having made an effort to practise these principles in all our affairs we tried to carry this message to other compulsive gamblers.** Action is the key word of this step. Here we turn to our fellow compulsive gambler who is still gambling. Here, we experience the kind of giving that asks no rewards.

There is great value in this step both in helping the newest member who is struggling to come to terms with their gambling, or in carrying the message to the wider community. I do not doubt that the real depth of the pain, the pleasure and the irresistible force of a gambling dependency is best understood by someone who has experienced it. This twelfth step gives the recovering gambler a role to play in helping others which in turn helps develop their own confidence and a belief that they are, after all, an achiever.

General Comments About the Twelve-step Programme

As an informed outsider I see that the GA twelve-step programme offers a very powerful framework within which a problem gambler can successfully address their dependency. However, for those who make it a lifetime commitment it does more than that – it gives them a purpose, a reason, a faith and a code of conduct all of its own.

It is a programme that works well for some, and for others a combination of attending GA and undergoing parallel treatment for the dependency is an effective combination (see Chapter 11).

GA members will tell you that compulsive gambling is a disease, and can never be cured. Total abstinence of all forms of gambling (for some even raffle tickets) is necessary for success. A lifelong commitment to the fellowship, and continued observance of the twelve steps is the only way of ensuring they do not return to gambling. Whilst I am not convinced that it is necessarily true that all problem gamblers need to observe lifelong abstinence, particularly if they break the dependency whilst they were still quite young, I would agree that the GA approach offers a code of conduct that for many serves them well throughout their life.

Gam-Anon

Alongside many GA groups there is a meeting for partners, parents, family and friends of problem gamblers. This is available whether or not the gambler is attending GA. These normally take place on the same day, at the same place, and the same time as the GA meeting, but in a separate room. The support they offer to these family members can help the gambler sustain their resolve to break the dependency. However, Gam-Anon does much more for the family member in helping to focus on how they have previously responded to the situation and how they can adapt their response in the future. It provides an opportunity for self-examination and adjustment, it gives strength to any changes they wish to make in their life with the gambler and, in many instances, in a wider context.

An idea of the value of Gam-Anon can by gained from the following contribution by 'Sue':

> Gam-anon is a fellowship for families of compulsive gamblers in which all who bear this burden can find understanding, warmth and friendship, as well as practical help and hope. Living with someone suffering from this addiction is a destroying experience. It is solitary too, because people find it impossible to speak to anyone about it. They feel no one else could possibly understand. For this reason we all came to our first Gam-Anon meeting desperate and ashamed, and were amazed to find an open door to a new life.
>
> Compulsive gamblers take their families with them down the road to destruction. Living for years with a compulsive gambler's lies and his inability to face up to responsibilities has led many to become so disturbed that they have sought psychiatric advice, and some have even attempted suicide. To such we say, please believe the impossible and come to us so that we may share freely with you the help we have freely received; and by which we exchanged an existence for a life. (*UK Forum Newsletter* 1994, pp. 8–9.)

The Purpose of Gam-Anon

The are three strands to the value of the Gam-Anon group. These are to help members to:

- understand the gambling addiction and how it affects both the gambler and themselves

- to think and act constructively by sharing experiences and making suggestions, thereby assisting in the process of rebuilding their life

- regain self-respect and self-confidence and to develop an assertive approach to their own lives

Providing Support

The first feeling experienced by anyone who goes to Gam-Anon is likely to be that of relief. They realise that they are not the only person facing this problem, that there are others who have also experienced the destruction of a gambling dependency, and that there is hope.

One of the first messages that the Gam-Anon group would wish to instil is that responsibility for the gambling lies with the gambler. The partner or parent should not feel guilty for the behaviour of the gambler and, that they are not a failure because their partner or child has become hooked on gambling. The Gam-Anon member is encouraged to accept only responsibility that they should rightly own.

A practical way the group can help is in bringing order to the chaos and panic that surrounds a mountain of debt and the pressure to respond to demanding creditors. Through shared experience, knowledge gained by other members and, on occasion, by help from a specific member to go through the debts, this seemingly insurmountable and terrifying problem can be reduced to a manageable size.

After relief, feelings of acute anger and resentment may well follow, and the group can help the member express them in a safe environment and then to work through and resolve them – and thus to move on.

The role that the Gam-Anon member has adopted in their relationship with the gambler is also explored. In many instances the excessive gambler has driven the parent or partner to adopt an extreme parenting or controlling stance. In my experience, particularly with parents, this stance has been adopted before the onset of the gambling and is probably a contributing factor in the gambler developing the dependency in the first place. However, the object of the group process is not to blame, it is rather to encourage the partner or parent to 'let go' and to give up control of the gambler. Bearing in mind the low self-esteem and feelings of worthlessness experienced by problem gamblers, a step in their recovery is to feel good about taking responsibility for their own lives. The Gam-Anon group can assist in this process by encouraging a parent to reformulate their relationship with a grown son or daughter, and a wife or husband to develop an equal role with their partner.

The solidarity that arises from sharing a common problem is a further source of strength for the parent or partner coming to terms with the dependency and its affects. They will hear that the recovery process is likely to take a long time and that there will be painful moments along the way both in sorting out the mess caused by the gambling and more importantly, in adjustments in their future relationship. The sense of belonging can have particular significance in the early months as it is very likely that the parent(s) or partner will have become isolated from friends and family. As they are able to reshape their life and mix with the wider community without fear or shame, Gam-Anon, for some, continues to provide an anchor of support.

The group can also be a source of strength and act as a sounding board when the situation continues to be intolerable and leads to the break-up of the relationship. This may occur either because the gambler continues with the activity or because the dynamics of change in their life together become too uncomfortable for one or more people involved.

SUMMARY

GA is a fellowship of men and women who share their experience, strength and hope with each other to solve their gambling problem and to help others to do the same. At the core of their approach is the twelve-step recovery programme. Gam-Anon, the 'sister' organisation, provides support and strength to the family and friends of problem gamblers.

CHECKLIST

The Value of Gamblers Anonymous

The fellowship of Gamblers Anonymous provides:

- A shared commonality in having experienced a dependency on gambling.

- Support and encouragement in coming to terms with their uncontrolled gambling and in stopping the activity.

- Help in maintaining a gambling-free lifestyle.

- Shared experience and advice to those who express a wish to stop gambling.

- A lifelong fellowship where recovering problem gamblers can feel they belong.

- A code of conduct for life that is constructive for the former gambler and for others with whom they have contact.

The Value of Gam-Anon

The related organisation Gam-Anon provides:

- A group where the destructive experience of another's gambling is understood and where there will be an empathetic response.

- A safe environment within which the deep emotions that have arisen by the affect of a gambling dependency can be openly expressed.

- Understanding the role a parent or partner has played in their relationship with the problem gambler and strengthening a resolve not to collude with the gambler's game-playing.

- An opportunity for sharing experiences and suggestions as to how an individual member can rebuild their life with or without the gambler.

- A source of help that enables a person affected by a gambling dependency to regain self-respect and self-confidence.

11 A Residential Approach

There is support and mutual responsibility,
you are helped and you help others.

(John – Gordon House resident, aged 44)

In the United Kingdom there are a handful of agencies that provide a residential facility for problem gamblers. However, these are few in number and tend to include gambling as a side issue that has arisen from their work with other dependencies. In this category I would include those that offer a private service, charging each resident between £1500 and £2000 per week, those that come under the provisions of the National Health Service or the judicial system, and those that are church-based. Extensively, but not exclusively, the approach applied to problem gamblers – as with residents experiencing other dependencies – is based around the twelve-step model outlined in Chapter 10.

One agency, however, stands out within the UK and, I believe, in Europe as the only specialised, long-term residential facility for problem gamblers. The Gordon House Association was established some 26 years ago. This chapter outlines the development and work of that association and describes the therapeutic programme that has evolved and which I believe provides a strong framework on which residents can rebuild their lives.

Why Was the Gordon House Association Established?

Gordon House is named after its founder the Reverend Gordon Moody who, after he had set up Gamblers Anonymous in the 1960s, responded to the urgent need to make provision for homeless and destitute problem gamblers. From the outset it was established as a charity and, in order to provide good-quality accommodation, has consistently worked in conjunction with voluntary sector Housing Associations. The first House was established in south London and opened its doors in 1971. From the beginning a strong link was established with the judiciary and it became a refuge for problem gamblers who were released or diverted from prison – the intention being to break the cycle of gambling–crime–imprisonment. The constitution required the Association to 'make provision to relieve the suffering and distress caused by compulsive gambling', and that remains the case to this day.

The Development of Gordon House

Over the years the regime has markedly changed and developed and, during my own long association with Gordon House, an expertise has evolved that has effectively helped hundreds of chronic problem gamblers.

Until a few years ago the House was financially supported by a direct Home Office grant which meant that admittance was restricted to ex-offenders whose criminality was directly related to problem gambling, and who expressed a serious intention to address the dependency. More recently that source of funding has been closed to Gordon House which, whilst it has contributed to financial uncertainty, has broadened the national catchment area to include referrals from a range of agencies or by self-referral from the problem gamblers themselves.

Ethos and Objectives

The ethos of this residential service has not changed from its beginning. It is available to any male problem gambler who is assessed as being suitable to take up residency. At one stage the House was available to both sexes but the predominance of men within the structure of the houses which the Association operate has caused it to restrict entry at the present time to males. As it is acutely conscious of the exclusivity of this policy at a time when female problem gambling is increasing, it is a matter that is under review.

The aim of the Association is to provide accountable services that reduce problem gambling and the harm done by such gambling. The objectives are to:

• provide support and effective residential therapies to those most affected by problem gambling

• provide, where possible and practicable, effective outreach for those waiting to join, or who have recently left, the residential programme

• undertake and facilitate reviews, studies and research that may lead to a better understanding of the nature and effects of problem gambling and its treatment

- provide, where possible and practicable, effective outreach and therapeutic interventions to those for whom the residential programme is not appropriate

- undertake tasks as an association, alone or in conjunction with others, that will reduce the harmful social impact of gambling.

The Programme

The programme was developed by Kevin Farrell-Roberts, the current project director, and is centred round a nine-month period of residency and support after which the gambler moves back into the wider community. Progression through the programme has been split into four distinct phases that are contained within a core therapeutic approach.

As a resident explained to me, Gordon House provides a structured programme that enabled him to re-establish a routine and then to understand his gambling and why he did it.

It provides a safe haven where the chaotic existence that the gambler has led can be left behind and he can begin to rebuild his life. As another resident explained, it can provide a place 'to hide'; the gambler can stop running and can, with help, develop the courage to face the mess that he has created. It enables him to take responsibility for himself *and* for others, thereby helping to restore self-esteem.

Core approach. Central to the programme is the group living experience where all residents share the same resolve. They support each other through the changes each of them has to make. By understanding through their own experience they can recognise and provide for each other's needs. Whilst any lapse back into gambling will come under close scrutiny, unless the resident is clearly demonstrating he does not want to address his problem, the examination is done in a supportive fashion. In the words of Fred, a resident at the house, 'When you have a lapse you can turn to other people for help, people who understand and to whom you can talk.'

Phase One: Coping with Today

After a three-month spell of stealing I was caught and remanded in custody. I was expecting 18 months inside. My solicitor had heard of a place which helped problem gamblers – the name of it being Gordon House. I passed the assessment and went back to court. By a miracle, I was given another chance, the judge said

that it was on my own initiative to help myself. Gordon House
is a shared House with twelve other residents. We have weekly
meetings about gambling and how things are going on. You must
have a serious commitment to give up gambling. I have been
here for three months, and have slipped up now and again, but I
have to expect the odd slip up now and again. Gambling cannot
be cured overnight, but it can be beaten and broken down. It is a
painful process and needs lots of help and support which I am
getting at the House. (Darren, aged 20)

This first stage is a combination of assessment and time management
skill training. New residents are assessed as to their motivation and
suitability for the programme. If they wish to continue with the
programme and are assessed as suitable, they undertake a life audit.
This examines in detail nine separate life areas:

• physical health

• emotional health

• beliefs and values

• social life

• relationships

• family issues

• legal issues

• education and career

• gambling history

This helps to identify not only what they have lost, but what they have
left to build upon. An action plan is then agreed that identifies when
and by what means each individual is going to address outstanding
issues, to achieve hopes and aspirations and to maintain a gambling-
free lifestyle.

    This plan, which is agreed as a contract, is compiled in conjunction
with a key worker and a consultant psychotherapist. During this phase
the resident completes a programme that is designed to focus on new,
or reawaken old, leisure pursuits. This is seen as particularly important as prior to coming to the House the gambler may well have spent
his waking day either gambling or planning his next session. Residents
describe the boring and depressing void created when they stop as the
'cold turkey' of giving up gambling.

Many new residents feel de-skilled or have never learnt how to cope in the community. It is during this phase that an element of skill training is introduced, either in conjunction with an outside agency or, when this clashes with the necessity of attending the Gordon House programme, through an in-house course. This helps to combat boredom and the onset of depression that is brought on by the realisation of what they have lost (in a wide sense) through gambling. It also gives them confidence to respond confidently to pressure from benefit agencies, family or creditors, to take paid employment, and for any return to a job to be planned in advance.

The other objective of Phase One is to re-establish a sense of stability in the life of the gambler. The mess he has left behind and the chaotic lifestyle he had recently been leading has to be addressed. Residency provides the opportunity to step away from the disorder and, together with the help of others, to bring it under control and to a manageable state. The new resident can also begin to feel a sense of security and well being simply by restoring a routine into his life. Living in a small residential community requires each resident to play a part in the running of the House and in looking after himself. During the term they stay at the House it is their home and residents are required to play a part in keeping it clean as well as taking part in House activities. They will have their own matters to sort out regarding their financial affairs, family matters, addressing any involvement in the legal or judicial system, registering with a local GP, employment issues, and many others. Whilst residents are encouraged to tackle any personal issues themselves, the fact that a designated support worker and other helpers are at hand to help, means that much of the fear and uncertainty of facing up to their difficulties is removed. This in itself has a value in beginning the restoration of self-esteem and establishing a sense of personal worth.

A particularly valuable support network of fellow residents is also established during this first phase. Being among others who understand something of what the gambler has experienced and have already moved through the stabilisation process is a tremendous help to the newcomer struggling to come to terms with his situation. At any stage during their stay at the House, residents might feel a strong urge to return to gambling. This is often felt particularly strongly during the initial few weeks. The companionship of another resident when the newcomer goes to pick up a social security benefit cheque, for instance, is cited as being a strong factor in preventing an early relapse.

Phase Two: Coping with Yesterday

> It has not been easy but the therapy meetings and support I receive from all the staff and other residents have really helped me. I have had two small bets since I have been here but for the first time in my life I know why I gamble, and this has played its part in stopping me from further gambling. I know now I have always gambled to hide from life because when I was gambling I did not have to do or think about anything else. I am really glad I came to Gordon House and am sorry that I did not come years ago. I have had a very sad life because of my gambling but, hopefully, by taking one day at a time and trying very hard not to give in I can have a happy and contented life without gambling. (George, aged 42)

Having successfully negotiated six weeks' settling in and being gambling-free the resident is ready to move on in the programme. Phase Two is the stage that has been described as the time when the 'real work' takes place. It is a three-month period where the gambler is provided with the opportunity to gain an insight as to why gambling became so important in his life. The resident joins a group whose focus is to explore the issues around gambling behaviour. During this part of the programme the resident also embarks on a twelve-week programme of individual counselling sessions. This personal focus is designed to explore the underlying factors for his dependency and likely reasons as to why he developed a gambling problem. At the end of the period a further review takes place. So as not to transfer dependency, to retain a focus on the cause and effect of gambling, and to use limited resources appropriately, the Association has evolved a clear policy to time-limit individual counselling. Should a need to explore other issues emerge or longer-term counselling appear desirable, the resident will be helped to get in touch with an appropriate counselling facility.

The Gordon House Association retains a positive link with the local Gamblers Anonymous group and residents are encouraged to attend. The value of how the two approaches work well in conjunction with one another is often appreciated by residents during this stage. They are able to make the connection between the support and resolve gained through the fellowship of GA with the understanding that comes from counselling undertaken at the House.

It is during this phase of their stay at Gordon House that many residents feel strong enough to begin to 'give back' after years of 'taking'. They will seek voluntary work, become involved in awareness-raising events or courageously share their story with the media, and begin to seek a rapprochement with their families. Such activities also provide a means of occupying their time in a far more positive fashion than previously.

Phase Three: Coping with Change and with Tomorrow

> At the age of 24 I broke into a house to get back the money I had lost on a previous gambling venture. This was to lead to one of the most frightening times of my life. Although I had a record for stealing, I had never before stood up in front of a judge. I began to realise how serious my gambling problem was ... Luckily for me the judge was lenient in giving me 18 months' probation and, shortly after, my application to Gordon House was accepted ... My life now, thanks to the House, has improved considerably and although it isn't easy coming to terms with what has happened in my life, I have refrained from gambling for six months now and am looking forward to living my life in a constructive way. (David, aged 25)

Those residents who have embraced and taken advantage of the first four and a half months of the programme are now ready to begin looking outward once again. The emphasis becomes that of developing those necessary strategies and skills so that they can move on in life without the desire to revert to a dependency on gambling. This is facilitated with a support group open to those who have reached this stage of their recovery. It provides a structured ten-week cycle of focused work that covers strategies to minimise a return to gambling, psychological and practical steps that the gambler can take if he does have a relapse and how Gordon House can help in the process.

For most, this means looking to a new career and lifestyle, based on either experience already gathered in their life or, for some, something completely different. Plans will be laid to return to their family area, to look for a fresh start somewhere else or to seek accommodation locally. There are a number of factors that dictate which of these options is pursued but the programme has been designed to facilitate whichever route is chosen. For example links have been established with local housing associations so that if the resident wishes to remain in the proximity of the House good quality accommodation can often be secured.

Meanwhile, at the south London location of the Association a second unit of three bedrooms allows these residents to move to a more independent situation and to relearn the skills needed for living in the wider community.

It is at this stage that residents will seek employment – the obtaining of which might influence the time when they leave the House. Some residents at this stage become impatient to move on and will choose to go before the expected period of residence. Others may not be ready to look outside the supportive and secure community to which they have become accustomed. They are likely to shy away from taking these steps towards independent living and their stay at the House may become extended.

> The depression of knowing I'd done my money once again clicked in my mind. I just walked away from everything again. I ended up in a homeless hostel until I got referred to Gordon House which gives you help, support and advice on how to cope with what has happened in your life and how to deal each day with our gambling problems. I've been here ten months now and have refrained from stealing and, most of all, from gambling. I now look forward to rebuilding my life with some independence and a gambling-free future. (Kevin, aged 30)

Residents are helped to secure accommodation, or to return to their family. Furniture may need to be purchased and other aspects of living in the wider community taken into consideration.

Phase Four: Coping on my Own

> When I was nearly 25 I found myself in court – yet again. I was given a probation order and moved into Gordon House the following week. I went through the programme, which was about a year in total. During this time I also went to Gamblers Anonymous and managed to abstain from gambling for a long time. I then moved into a flat and was doing well but it was not long before I started gambling again ... After gambling for a few more years I managed to take myself back to Gordon House for help and advice. This was the best move I could have made because I was taken back into the House. The main difference was that they now have a pool of qualified counsellors for individual counselling ... Because I was able to talk about my feelings and problems I have managed to believe in myself again and build up my self-esteem. I have got to say 'thank you' to my counsellor, and also hope that all problem gamblers get the chance of counselling like I have, because I personally know it works. (Michael, aged 33)

For the first three months after leaving the House, intensive outreach support, further group work and, in some instances, counselling are available. For those ex-residents that move some distance away the level of 'after care' is not as high as those that live locally. Nevertheless, they are encouraged to keep in touch and, when practical, support is offered.

A high proportion of residents decide to settle locally when they leave in order to avail themselves of the ongoing support provided by Gordon House and by each other. The intensive outreach support is phased out but continued contact with the House is encouraged. The ex-residents themselves have formed their own support group and a number of them continue their link with the local branch of Gamblers Anonymous.

Should an ex-resident be unable to cope in the wider community without returning to uncontrolled gambling, they are at liberty to apply for re-entry. Because of the demand on the small number of beds available, any such requests are assessed in the light of their application and their current motivation to change.

What it Gives to Residents

Monitoring has revealed that residents derive real value by staying in a safe and supportive environment among others who understand the dependency and within which their problem gambling can be addressed. The most highly-rated aspects of living at Gordon House are perceived as being:

- Socialising with and receiving day-to-day support from other residents.

- Individual sessions with designated support workers and provision by them of day-to-day support.

- Group meetings to share information, views and to explore issues.

- Individual counselling sessions.

(Farrell-Roberts 1997)

As in any therapeutic community the help it can offer to residents is affected by the mix of people going through the programme. Gordon House is no exception and a negative attitude displayed by a couple of residents can erode the efforts to break the dependency on gambling. However, this residential facility providing specialised individual help has an important place in the national network of services that assists those affected by a gambling dependency.

SUMMARY

The Gordon House Association was founded in the early 1970s and is the only specialised long-term residential facility for problem gamblers in the UK. The aim of the Association is to provide accountable services that reduce problem gambling and the harm done by such gambling. Their approach centres on a structured four-phase programme that covers assessment, insight, behaviour modification and a planned return to independent living.

CHECKLIST

The stages of the residential programme provided by the Gordon House Association are:

- **The Core** of the programme is the group living experience where all residents share the same resolve.

- **Phase One: coping with today** is a combination of assessment and time management skill training.

- **Phase Two: coping with yesterday** provides, through group work and individual counselling, an opportunity to explore underlying problems and reasons for the gambling dependency.

- **Phase Three: coping with change and with tomorrow** looks to develop the necessary strategies and skills to move on to a life without a gambling habit and to address the practicalities of returning to the wider community.

- **Phase Four: coping on my own** provides a decreased level of support while former residents establish themselves back into society.

12   Working with the Family

Advice to a family member: 'You can take the initiative for change. Change yourself not the gambler. Clear your head and concentrate on regaining your confidence. Stop behaving like a puppet on a string and find your own independent person. Allow the gambler to take responsibility for his addiction and the problems it is causing.'

(Moody 1990, p. 48)

Working with the problem gambler in isolation is in many instances a necessity of situation or circumstances. However, where it is possible to involve the gambler's parent or partner a number of advantages may be attained. It will not be possible to do full justice in the space available to this specialised form of counselling, so in this chapter I will simply highlight some of the factors that should be taken into consideration when working with the family of a problem gambler.

Understanding the Problem

The family member whose life has been affected by the dependency is very often at a loss to understand the power of the addiction. Including them in the counselling process, particularly when the gambler talks about what they have done and what drove them to do it, is likely to increase the understanding of the family member. This in turn can assist them to realise that, whilst there might be aspects of their own relationship that are linked to the gambler and their behaviour, they are not responsible for the addiction. By involving the family member the counsellor is likely to gain a deeper understanding of the dynamics that affect the gambler, and which aspects within the relationship between the gambler and the family member are having a significant impact on the dependency.

Understanding the Process

By attending with the gambler the family member can begin to appreciate the process of the counselling for themselves. This is likely to provide a better understanding than hearing of it second-hand through the inevitably distorted report of the gambler. This is particularly so of parents who having quizzed their son or daughter pick up a picture that they cannot understand. For example, take the issue of confidentiality. In my experience, parents of adolescents in particular have demanded to know what was said in a counselling session. They have telephoned angrily accusing the counsellor of colluding with the gambler's secrecy and of usurping their parental authority in instances where the gambler has avoided responding to the curiosity of their parent by citing the bounds of confidentiality. The other aspect in understanding the process is that of gaining not only their acceptance but also their involvement. There will be a range of issues that they as well as the gambler will need to address during the period of time that the gambling dependency is addressed.

Involvement in the Process

It is more difficult for the family member to remain in their own cosy area of denial if they have become involved in the treatment process. The partner who takes the stance with the gambler that 'It's your problem, you sort it out', is probably making recovery more difficult for the gambler and the chances of their relationship surviving the transition away from dependency that much more unlikely. Whilst involvement of the family member may, at the beginning, feed into any co-dependency (for example, sick-person–nurse roles) their involvement allows the counsellor to address this dynamic at an appropriate time. Working at the problem, however it is defined, together can greatly strengthen the resolve to carry on, be the means of strong support should a lapse occur, and provide the basis for a sense of mutual satisfaction once the dependency has been overcome. This, in fact, occurs within the GA/Gam-Anon approach even though the people concerned do not attend the same meeting.

Involving a Parent

By the time a young problem gambler is willing to look at their dependency it is likely that a degree of havoc will have taken place within the home as a result of the gambling. The parent is likely to be wrestling with a variety of emotions which will almost certainly include those of anger, sadness, puzzlement and guilt. It is very likely that the initial contact with the agency was made by the parent following the discovery of, or a marked escalation in, the destructive impact of the gambling dependency on the family.

They may well be devastated and it is important that, even before contact is made with the gambler, the parent should be enabled to understand the situation.

Some while ago I drew up the following list of points that it would be appropriate to share with a parent either during or as a follow-up to their initial contact. This has now been incorporated into *Young Gambling: A Guide for Parents* (Bellringer and Farman 1997):

- Remember that you are not the only family facing this problem.

- You may be able to help your child by talking the problem through but it is probably better if a skilled person outside the family is also involved.

- Keep in mind that it is a serious matter and the gambler cannot 'just give up'.

- Take a firm stand; whilst it might feel easier to give in to demands and to believe everything they say, this allows your son or daughter to avoid facing the problem.

- Remember that your child likes to gamble and is getting something from the activity quite apart from money.

- Do not forget that gamblers are good at lying – to themselves as well as to you.

- Let your son or daughter know that you believe it is a problem even though they may not admit it.

- Encourage your child all the time as they have to be motivated to change.

- Be prepared to accept that your son or daughter may not be motivated to change until they are faced with an acute crisis.

- Leave the responsibility for the gambling and its consequences with the gambler, but also help them to face up to it and to work at overcoming the dependency.

- Do not condemn them, as it is likely to be unhelpful and may drive them further into gambling.

- Setting firm and fair boundaries for your child's behaviour is appropriate and is likely to be constructive in providing a framework with which to address the dependency.

- Despite what your son or daughter may have done it is important to let them know that you still love them. This should be done even if you have to make a 'tough love' decision such as asking them to leave home.

- Do not trust them with money until the dependency has been broken. If they are agreeable it is a helpful strategy for a defined, short period of time to manage their money for them.

I have known parents who, having made this initial contact, then distance themselves from the process of recovery. However, it is more common that they wish to be further involved. The underlying attitude of the parent can at this early stage become apparent and can provide some strong indicators as to the family dynamics that have had an influence on the gambler. The checklist of predisposing factors described earlier in the book (see Chapter 4) may usefully be kept in mind during early contact with a parent. However, it is just as likely that there are no readily apparent attitudinal clues as to why the gambler became vulnerable to a dependency on gambling. The involvement of the parent, particularly in the initial stages, is important and useful in obtaining a broad picture and securing their appropriate assistance in the recovery process. On the other hand, when dealing with young problem gamblers going through the phases of transition from child to adult, it is just as important to value and respect the young person's need for individual attention outside the family.

It is useful to keep in mind the following when involving the parent of a problem gambler.

Comfort. Check out at an early stage how comfortable the gambler is likely to feel if one or both parents are involved, and also how comfortable the parents may feel.

Assessment. Unless sufficient information has been obtained at the point of initial contact, it would be useful to carry out an assessment interview with the parent or guardian. This should be (at least partly) separate from that conducted with the young gambler to facilitate an environment where each can talk freely and feel a sense of personal value. Combining this with a joint assessment is likely to provide a good idea of the dynamics between parent and child.

Single/Joint sessions. Whilst circumstances may vary from case to case it is probable that with a young problem gambler a mixture of single and joint sessions will be appropriate. Because of the need for the problem gambler to feel valued in their own right I would suggest a number of individual sessions with the young person should take place before a parent is jointly involved.

Sensitivity. Each may need reminding of the other's vulnerability and sensitivity of feelings. The young gambler may have the perception, real or imagined, that they are not treated fairly, are not loved, or are put upon. The parent may feel taken advantage of, that their feelings and views are ignored by their child, may feel guilty or misunderstood, or feel that the care they have given their child is discounted. This may particularly be the case if it is a single-parent family or the parent requesting help feels isolated within the family.

Respect and valuing. Whilst it is likely to take a long time before a high degree of trust is restored in the gambler it is clearly helpful to focus on rebuilding respect and in valuing each other's qualities and attributes. This enables the parent to adjust to a more constructive perspective of their child, and the young gambler to recognise that the concern is genuine and that their parent is trying to be supportive.

Control. There will almost certainly be issues of control around in the interaction between the young gambler and the parent(s). A father might manifest this in attempting to set rigid and inappropriate boundaries whilst a mother might display signs of being over-protective. Parental control may well have contributed to the creation of the gambling dependency as the son or daughter sought to escape, to feel power for themselves or to rebel against an oppressive value system. Quite obviously these issues require sensitive handling as the young gambler may exaggerate the effect, and the parent may resent the very suggestion that they have contributed to the excessive gambling. As it is an issue for thousands of families during the phase of shifting teenager–parent relationships it can be broached in this general context before relating specifically to the gambling.

Letting go. Linked to the issue of control is, of course, a change required in the parent. Letting their 'child' go, allowing their son or daughter the space to take responsibility for their own actions, making that leap of faith that this young person can think through a situation and make their own decisions, is a big deal for most parents. In the instance of a young problem gambler it is quite likely to have increased significance but needs to be addressed and may provide the key to change.

Understanding. There is likely to be a breakdown of understanding between the generations. This will probably be more than the puzzlement that we all face when trying to come to terms with the generation gap. The parent is unlikely to understand why their son or daughter plays slot machines or buys scratchcards, especially if gambling holds no interest for them. Conversely, the young gambler will not understand why the obvious pleasure that they experience from gambling is not appreciated by their parent(s). Encouraging the young person to talk about what they feel and asking the parent actively to listen should improve understanding.

Responsibility. Both parent and gambler need to accept responsibility for the process and consequence of change. Addressing the gambling is likely to expose underlying reasons for the dependency which can come as a considerable shock. That this may happen should be pointed out from the start and responsibility accepted. Should the change include the parent letting go, it is important to help prepare the gambler and the parent for this step towards maturation.

Encouragement. Filling the void created by the cessation of gambling is an essential part of breaking the dependency. The development of other interests may be simply a case of picking up where the gambler left off. However, it is more probable that considerable time, effort and possibly money will be involved in finding pastimes that meet similar needs. It is important that the parent encourages and supports these efforts as far as they are able to do so.

Gambling focus. It is quite likely that counselling will highlight other underlying problems that have in part contributed to the dependency. Whilst the sensitive exploration of these may be within the remit of the counselling programme, generally speaking the focus on gambling should not be lost. In the case of multiple addiction, or disclosure of serious traumatic experience – especially abuse – these issues would also need to be addressed.

Involving a Partner

> The challenge to the couples therapist is to move beyond the goal of helping the couple become a functional unit to the goal of creating an intimate relationship through resolution of long-term emotional issues and changing dysfunctional interactions which prevent relationship growth. (M.A. Steinberg 1993, p. 2)

This may well be possible in an agency that caters for longer-term intervention, but when sessions are limited the focus should remain on breaking the dependency on gambling and how the couple can achieve that together.

The partner of the problem gambler may not be aware of the full extent of the debts, the lying and the desperate acts that have been carried out. Having ascertained that the problem gambler wants their partner involved it is important that they are encouraged to tell them the whole story. Of course there is risk attached to this strategy but not nearly as much as when the gambler continues to hide and, inevitably, to lie to their partner. Having experienced the devastation of the gambling dependency and listened to the gambler's story it is probable that all semblance of trust by the partner will have disappeared. However, if the couple genuinely wish to work at the situation together the partner has to take a risk in according an element of trust.

Issues around finances are likely to be central to the early discussions and, unless this can be addressed within the parameters of the counselling sessions, may well require a referral to an appropriate debt counselling agency. Until the panic and fear of a pressing debt can be brought under control it is unlikely that either partner will be able to concentrate on other issues.

Confidence levels in both of them are likely to be low and there is a strong case for the partner's needs in this regard to also be addressed. In the case of a male problem gambler the partner's self-esteem is likely to have suffered as she sees the gambling placed before his love for her. Self-doubt about her own worth and what she must do to recapture his love will have begun to preoccupy her. She is likely to have adopted one of the following roles.

The Martyr. In this situation the female adopts a role of long suffering and acceptance of her lot. Basically she allows the gambler to control the situation and manages to survive by getting what she can from him or, alternatively, finding other resources to call upon. She makes little attempt to stop his behaviour but blunts the effect as much as possible. The Martyr may well seek consolation in religion or in a group of people with whom she has some status. In this way she manages to retain some dignity and meets the essential criterion in a relationship – that of being needed. It does not help the gambler address his problem, however, as he can carry on his activity without having to account for his actions or face a crisis within the home.

Feeling needed is likely to be the key when the gambler and his partner express a wish to work together to overcome the dependency. The gambler wants to feel he is needed by his partner and has a positive role to play within the family. Conversely, the partner will expect to feel needed by the gambler and that she has ousted gambling in his affections. A focus on interdependent need is likely to help the gambler and the Martyr work effectively together.

The Mother. Helping the gambler is at the core of this role. The wife or female partner colludes with the gambler in order to save and protect him. She will excuse his behaviour to herself, her family and to the outside world. When able she is likely to bail him out financially and may even saddle herself with financial agreements on his behalf. His needs get put before her own and those of the children. The Mother is likely to collude to the extent of lying to other members of the family and to outsiders. By adopting this attitude to the gambler the wife can feel in control and able to express and receive love within their relationship. This behaviour only serves to give approval to the gambler and helps him justify his behaviour. He can continue to avoid responsibility knowing that in a crisis he can call upon his wife for support.

In this situation a redistribution of love is required. The partner must shed responsibility for the gambling by not colluding, no longer pretending to believe his lies and tall stories. It is probable that by agreeing to become involved in counselling sessions it feeds her need to be the 'rescuer'. This is a role that needs to be avoided. Working out the future together at an adult-to-adult level should help the restoration, or creation, of a more balanced partnership.

The Malcontent. This is a role adopted by the wife to take back control and as a means of wresting back some of the power held by the gambler. She will become deeply critical of him, belittling everything he does and undermining him at every opportunity. She will openly express a mistrust of him and will put him down in front of the children or other family members she sees as allies. She will check up on him constantly and hound him whenever she thinks he is gambling. Her interest in him and in a positive relationship dwindles or disappears altogether, and she may seek solace in other relationships, religion or a different addiction, such as alcohol. This, of course, is likely to exacerbate the gambler's low opinion of himself and drive him deeper into the comfort of gambling.

The problem gambler–Malcontent is perhaps the least likely partnership to survive. It will depend heavily on what the partner still has invested in the relationship and how she can cope with a 'reformed' gambler. The balance of control is an important element in restoring the basis to face change together.

Counselling the Partner of a Problem Gambler

There are a number of factors that it is important to consider when working with the partner or someone close to the problem gambler, including the following:

The state of the relationship. Asking questions, listening and observing how the two people inter-react will all help in building up a picture of their relationship. This should help decide which, if any, of the categories detailed above are appropriate to the partner. However, as always, great caution should be taken to avoid attaching labels to anyone and it is likely that they may exhibit traits of character that fit all three or, indeed, do not belong to any category. What is important is to ascertain as clearly as possible the dynamics of the relationship between the couple. It is probably best to do so at the assessment stage as it will help everyone decide how to progress the sessions.

Single or together. It may be that the couple, or one of them, make the decision about this very clear. It is equally likely that they will seek a lead from the counsellor. If the gambler appears to have genuinely shared the full extent of the gambling and they are both aware of the difficulties facing them, couple counselling from the beginning may be appropriate. If this is not the case subsequent sessions may be side-tracked to explore aspects of their relationship to one another that move the focus completely away from gambling. Should the counsellor have the time to explore some of these other important issues this may be very beneficial. If not, it may be better to see the gambler alone for a while before introducing the partner.

Feelings. For each to understand how gambling makes the other feel it would be of value to explore this in some detail. As the gambler tells their story, a check on how the other felt may come as a revelation to the gambler. Equally, actions by the partner that precipitated further gambling or thoughts about doing so provide insight as to the triggers that made the gambler particularly vulnerable.

Responsibility. Accepting responsibility for one's own actions is, of course, an important aspect of seriously addressing a gambling dependency. Without doing so it is unlikely that the gambler will stop, neither will it allow them to break away from being dependent. The role of the partner is partly to refuse to take responsibility for the gambling and partly to accept responsibility for their own actions. Whilst in many instances something is done or said as a direct result of a gambling session or its consequences, it also becomes a conven-ient 'whipping boy' on which to heap blame for every mistake or adverse occurrence. Differentiating which is attributable to the gam-bler and which to the partner may be tricky but is important in the process of valuing each other.

Co-dependency. The 'mothering' role described earlier may well have been a factor at the beginning of the relationship – meeting the needs of both people concerned. It may also have developed as a result of the gambling causing the partner to adopt a stance in order to survive. This would be equally true for other adopted roles such as ascribing a 'sick' role to the gambler. The information gained at the time of assessment should have provided some clues but it would be worth returning to the subject of co-dependency within joint counselling. It may be that even when the gambling dependency has been broken, a strength in the relationship remains that of co-dependency and this should be acknowledged. It might also be the case that having affected change in the behaviour of the gambler it provides a catalyst for a different shared relationship in the future. Both gambler and partner need to be aware of this possibility.

Support. Encouragement and support are vital ingredients to restoring self-esteem and boosting confidence. This is likely to apply as much to the partner as it is to the gambler so that they should be given the opportunity to explore ways in which they may give support and encouragement to one another. This in itself is likely to allow each to see the other in a new light and to do much to restore their faith in the value of human relationships – replacing for the gambler a need for a strong attachment to the machine, the casino or the betting office, and reassuring the partner that they are loved.

SUMMARY

Whilst not always possible, it is an advantage to involve the problem gambler's partner or parent(s) in the process of encouraging change. Their inclusion helps them understand the problem and increases their involvement in breaking the dependency. If it is a parent who is involved the focus may be on letting their child become more independent. With a partner, on the other hand, the concentration may well centre on re-establishing their relationship with the gambler.

CHECKLIST

Working with family members when addressing a gambling dependency can markedly enhance the chances for successful intervention. Most commonly, the involvement will be with a parent or with the partner of the gambler.

Involving a Parent

When talking to a parent about their involvement in the process of change, it is of value to include the following points:

- Remember you are not alone.
- Involve a skilled person outside the family to help.

- The gambler cannot simply 'give up' the gambling.
- Be aware that their son or daughter likes to gamble.
- Take a firm stand – do not collude with the gambler.
- They lie to themselves as well as to you.
- Let them know that *you* see it as a problem.
- Encourage them to change.
- Accept that their motivation to change may only come after an acute crisis.
- Leave responsibility for the gambling with the gambler.
- Do not condemn them for their addiction.
- Set firm and fair boundaries.
- Let your son or daughter know that you still love them.
- Do not trust them with money until the dependency has been broken.

Involving a partner

When planning to undertake work with a problem gambler and their partner it is useful to keep in mind the following points:

- Build up a picture of their relationship by questioning, listening and observing.
- Check their preference to be seen singly or jointly.
- Help them to understand how gambling makes each of them feel.
- Encourage both of them to accept responsibility for their own actions.
- Identify what aspects of co-dependency are apparent in the relationship.
- Explore with them ways in which they might support and encourage each other through the change process.

13 Problem Prevention

Responsibility for the effects of gambling is one that must be shared by all of us ... Between us we need to take particular care in respect of the small minority who either engage in excessive gambling or have problems as a result of their activity.

(Chris Bell, MD Ladbroke Racing, 1998)

To quote an old adage, the best means of cure is prevention. Many problem gamblers will forcefully express an opinion that the best means of prevention would be to prohibit all forms of gambling. Whilst I understand the reason for this sentiment it is neither sensible nor practical. Prohibition of anything that meets strongly felt needs of human beings is doomed to failure – and gambling is no exception to this rule.

By far the best approach is to ensure that legislation and regulation take due regard of the need to prevent problems. Those involved in promoting gambling need to be encouraged or otherwise persuaded to do so in a manner that minimises harm. An education message needs to be delivered that gives everyone who gambles the opportunity to do so from informed choice, and for those that have a community advisory role to understand the issues. Treatment programmes that support relapse prevention need to be devised for those harmed by gambling. Let us look at these strands in more detail.

Legislation and Regulation

It has long been recognised that controls over gambling are necessary. The reasons for this are threefold.

First, it is an activity that is attractive to those who are of criminal intent. Although the situation is gradually changing, the monetary transaction involved in gambling is usually by means of cash – creating an ideal route for laundering 'hot' money. The unscrupulous operator can easily exploit the gambler by, for example, obscuring the payout margin, taking an extortionate percentage of the stake and prize from the winner, using crooked means of conducting the gambling activity, or by stealing back money that has been won.

Second, gambling and religion have always had an uneasy relationship. Indeed, as mentioned in Chapter 1, some creeds such as the Muslim faith consider gambling to be evil and prohibit adherents from such activities. The Christian faiths are more equivocal even though the church has often gained huge benefit from encouraging or, at least, tolerating gambling. However, the influence of the prevailing religious faith both in the UK and elsewhere has been a strong voice in highlighting the need to consider the moral and ethical rightness of allowing widespread gambling. This has had a marked affect in shaping legislation and the interpretation of regulation.

Third, it is an activity where the participants need to some extent to be protected from themselves. It is outside the scope of the book to argue the merits of whether the state should intervene at all as long as the transaction takes place within proscribed legal limits. However, gambling can become such an attraction as to cause otherwise quite conservative people to over-extend themselves and to get carried away in the heat of the moment. The value placed on money in society; the status that can be obtained from being a big winner or, indeed, a 'cool loser'; the powerful need in some to 'chase a dream' of instantly changing their lifestyle for something better can all combine with the excitement of taking a risk to cause them to throw caution to the wind.

Having established reasons for regulation it is also important to legislate carefully. Loopholes in the law can and will be exploited. We do not have to go back too far in time for an example of how the failure to regulate properly quickly led to huge problems, as the following quote illustrates.

The Betting and Gaming Act of 1960 aimed to continue prohibition as far as gaming was concerned (although not with regard to betting) apart from some small-scale gaming in members clubs, for worthy causes (this was known as the 'Vicar's Charter'), and in other ways no doubt considered harmless. However the drafters got it monumentally and disastrously wrong as far as gaming was concerned. It caused or permitted chaos, violence and extortion, and led to a powerful public outcry against gaming ... So what happened? Of course commercial gaming flourished. According to the 1976 Royal Commission on Gambling, 'casinos were flourishing like weeds in many parts of the country'. By 1968 there were some 1200 casinos ... There were gambling junkets from abroad, the gamblers being brought over by special charter flights. There were frequent protection rackets, associated both with casinos and more particularly with machines. For example, the proprietors of some boarding houses were forced to have machines on their premises by criminals, and organised crime took a large slice of the profit ... Naturally organised crime became very heavily involved, both our home-grown variety as well as Mafia. Blackmail and violence were used to enforce gambling debts. (FitzGerald 1994, p. 29)

Incidentally, that experience led to the much better-drafted Gaming Act of 1968. The number of gaming establishments dropped by 90 per cent, and the casino became the most tightly regulated form of gambling in the UK – a situation that holds to the present day.

This 1968 Act also created the Gaming Board for Great Britain as a government-appointed regulator not only for casinos but also for bingo clubs and gaming machines. In 1976 lotteries were added to this portfolio of responsibilities, although the National Lottery is separately regulated by the National Lottery Commission (NLC). The regulation of betting has remained under direct Home Office control.

The experience of the 1960 disaster also had a strong influence on government thinking for the next 30 years. From the 1968 Act onwards legislation worked on the principle of demand not being stimulated and any concession to gambling was hemmed in by tight regulation. Strangely, however, low-payout gambling machines, known as Amusement With Prizes (AWP) machines, escaped severe stricture. Inexplicably, the danger of this potentially addictive form of gambling was overlooked to the extent that no minimum age restriction was imposed and they can be seen to this day in a whole range of non-specific gambling venues, such as cafes and fish and chip shops.

Apart from the recent National Lottery Act of 1993, gambling for the twenty-first century is governed by legislation that is becoming increasingly inadequate and out of date. It is time for a review of gambling and amendment to legislation to reflect modern trends and technological advance. A good framework of regulation coupled with a government willingness to pay serious regard to social aspects of gambling will do much to ensure that preventative measures will be effective. It is vital that society as a whole, having embraced gambling more enthusiastically than ever before, does not lose sight of the need to ensure adequate preventative steps are taken to minimise harm.

There is also a need to distinguish between the various forms of gambling that are on offer and regulate according to their potential to cause problems. At one end of the continuum are to be found *soft* forms of gambling such as the football pools or the twice-weekly draw for the National Lottery (that is, discontinuous forms of gambling where there are only one or two gambles per week). At the other end are the 'hard' forms such as slot machines or the roulette wheel. Some of the defining features of a gambling activity at the harder end of the spectrum include:

- **Rapid event frequency** – for example, the roulette wheel spins for 20–30 seconds which allows a number of games to be played in rapid succession.

- **Memory period of loss is brief** – for instance, concentrating on the hands at the blackjack table pushes the memory of previous losses to the back of the mind, particularly if the player has a mixture of winning and losing hands.

- **Potential for continual interaction** – for instance, the betting office provides an interactive environment where you can study form, place your bet, watch the action and collect or try again.

- **Potential for chasing losses in a single session** – for instance, the slot machine with its rapid play provides the opportunity for losses to be chased for as long as the player has money to feed into the machine.

- **Variable stake** – for example, there are a whole range of betting opportunities at the racecourse from singles to multiples and from very small stakes to significant sums of money. This can encourage a player to stay at the activity for longer and to adjust their stake according to their reasoning and money available.

- **Money can be quickly reinvested** – for example, buying and rubbing off scratchcards at the point of sale enables the player to immediately reinvest any winnings.

It will be noticed that no mention is made of the amount that can be won. The gain is a significant factor in initially attracting someone to gamble but the development and maintenance of a hard form of gambling is more due to psychological and physiological factors (Griffiths 1995). Staying at the activity for as long as possible in order to escape, to feel in control, and for the excitement of the 'action' of gambling, is more important. Any winnings are likely to be re-staked as a means of prolonging involvement. It is those 'hard' gambling activities which largely fit this description that are far more likely to lead to the development of a dependency on gambling.

In order to minimise the proliferation of problem gambling, regulations that concern 'hard' gambling need to be tighter and more restrictive than those at the other end of the continuum.

The Gambling Industry

Since I have been interested in the social impact of gambling I have noticed a significant shift in attitude by many organisations that include gambling in their portfolio of business affairs. In the past, the attitude of some sections within the gambling industry has been that their business activities were not the cause of problems and those who became addicted to gambling were simply 'sick' people.

Thankfully, that attitude is being replaced with a recognition that gambling can be the cause of very severe problems for a small minority of those who participate in the activity. Those members of the gambling industry that accept a 'duty of care' and positively respond to harm minimisation do much to assist problem prevention.

One reason for this, I am convinced, is that the legitimisation of gambling and the strengthening of senior management with younger and forward-thinking personnel have combined to reduce the previous attitude of embattled defence. The phrase I am beginning to hear is, 'It is not that we ought to do something, it is right that we do so.' There are, I would argue, a number of sound advantages for a company in the gambling business to develop problem prevention policies.

- Being seen to have a balanced approach that fulfils the obligation towards a duty of care and provides real evidence that its response goes beyond 'lip service' makes sound business sense.

- Benefits can be gained from a markedly positive improvement of company image. Acknowledging that its product can have a harmful consequence for a minority of gamblers and acting to minimise that harm can provide a strong counterweight to any accusations of exploitation.

- Company policy can be developed in the knowledge that ceasing to deny the existence of problem gambling does not pose a threat to the 'bottom line'. A caring image is likely to be seen by many customers as a reason for doing business with the company.

- The fact that the company is striving to find a balance and that it does care about social impact issues can be used as a significant strand in its marketing strategy. Furthermore, endorsement is likely to be forthcoming from other agencies including those who work with the social aspects of gambling.

- A balanced approach and a genuine care for vulnerable customers is likely to make staff feel more comfortable, particularly those who have face-to-face contact with punters they know to have problems or whose families are suffering.

- Incorporating harm minimisation considerations into the design and promotion of new or revamped products could mean that they are more likely to be looked upon favourably by the regulator.

- The acute financial penalties that could accrue from a standpoint of denial, should evidence of harm caused be proven, can be avoided. Whilst suppression or denial of information might bring short-term gain it could bring long-term disaster for the company.

It is, of course, a balancing act for those in the industry. Answerable to their shareholders, they are driven to maximise opportunity and to exploit the market whenever they can. On the other hand, the advantages in adopting a harm minimisation strategy should also be taken into consideration. The following list of measures that a gambling company might legitimately take provides, I would suggest, a good balance between apparently conflicting goals. They are also likely to contribute to problem prevention.

Product promotion. Care should be taken to develop promotional campaigns that do not mislead in terms of chances of winning. Neither should they be directed at inappropriate sections of the community, as was the first television advert for the National Lottery. This included a clip of a ten-year-old girl mesmerised by the magic, star-spangled hand – an incentive for this age group to become interested in a product that is, in fact, restricted to those aged 16 and over. The inclusion, in a promotion, of a cautionary note emphasising the need to keep gambling under control would do much to communicate a balanced message and would stimulate healthy interest in the gambling product. Virginia Bottomley, Minister of State for the then Department of Heritage in the 1993 Conservative Government, did a great disservice to public perception when she described the National Lottery as 'not really gambling at all but just a harmless flutter'.

Point of sale encouragement. Quite clearly, any vendor has a duty to encourage someone to make a purchase and to provide positive information about their products. This is entirely reasonable with gambling as with anything else, both in terms of company advertising and point of sale contact. However, in addition to the point about not providing false or misleading information, the need for harm minimisation needs to be kept in mind. Gamblers should not therefore be encouraged to stake more than they want to commit, should not be enticed to re-stake their winnings and, perhaps most importantly of all, should be discouraged from chasing losses.

Minimising illegal sales. The most obvious illegality which has attracted much regulatory and media interest in the last few years is that of under-age sales of gambling products. Young teenagers are particularly vulnerable and significant problem prevention can be achieved if age limits are taken seriously by the gambling company and effective control measures are introduced. The most effective measure is that of requiring proof of age to be produced in all cases where the vendor has doubts as to whether the customer is old enough. For some years the Portman Group has encouraged members of the alcohol trade to use its 'prove it' card as a means of determining that a young-looking customer is indeed 18 or over. This scheme has now been superseded by 'Citizen Card', a voluntary age-validation card that can cover a wide range of applications across an age-span from 12 to 21. Clearly, such a card can be used to check the age and identity of prospective gambling customers.

There are other positive measures that can be taken to minimise illegal sales; for example, appropriate signs, suitable publicity delivered at local community level, and staff training to emphasise the importance of the issues and instruction as to how to handle these customers.

A further harm minimisation measure comes into play when fraudulent or illegal purchases are attempted by customers – many of these would be potential or actual problem gamblers. Good security measures with regard to both deterrence and detection can be of great assistance in reducing the incidence of attempted fraud.

Unequivocal signage. Because of the regulations governing gambling activities and the inherent risk of forming a dependency it is most important that all venues that sell gambling products prominently display easily readable signs highlighting regulations that need to be brought to the customers' attention. In addition to emphasising an age restriction, such signs also provide an excellent opportunity to draw attention to the need to keep gambling under control or to refer customers to an available leaflet that gives this sort of information.

Getting help. Whilst only a small minority of gamblers get into difficulty, the number is significant and they are particularly susceptible to seeking advice when they have just sustained a heavy loss. The prominent display of a telephone 'hotline' number, included with other signage or, preferably, displayed separately in large, clear, eye-catching print provides a particularly valuable contribution to minimising further harm. The experience of the GamCare helpline (see Chapter 15) when a leaflet and the telephone number were first introduced into betting offices in 1998, was to record an immediate and noticeable increase in callers who felt they had or might have a problem because of their liking for betting.

Responsible play. A booklet or leaflet that covers the pleasures of gambling and describes the 'how' of taking part in a particular gamble provides a valuable service for customers, especially those who gamble infrequently or are just beginning to get involved. This is also an excellent medium for highlighting the risks of gambling and encouraging gamblers to take seriously the message that to maximise enjoyment and prevent problems they should be conscious of the need to keep their gambling under control. Easy accessibility of such information would be a crucial factor as to whether it is read or not. Having to ask for such a leaflet is likely to deter the very gamblers it is designed to reach – young people and those with mental health problems, for example.

Staff training. Any organisation that seriously wishes to contribute to problem prevention needs to ensure that it is a policy that is clearly known to and owned by staff. The inclusion of social impact issues in appropriate training sessions as well as being written into induction and other training manuals would positively encourage understanding and acceptance. Staff should be trained in dealing with gamblers who express a desire to be 'self-barred' from a gambling venue, and to be able to refer to an appropriate source family members who express concern. Whilst I acknowledge the delicacy of a member of staff being proactive in discouraging a known problem gambler, it is a step that I believe is achievable in certain circumstances. It is part of the policy of some overseas operators – Hurrahs in the US, for example, and should be tried out selectively in the UK.

Company commitment. Supporting and maintaining a dialogue at local and national level with reputable organisations that address social impact issues further demonstrates duty of care and is likely to contribute to problem prevention. This is particularly true of those organisations that consult with such agencies as to the design and promotion of existing and new products, and who work with them to create the signage and literature mentioned above. In my experience of working with the betting and gaming industry over a number of years I am detecting signs that sections of the industry are at last moving towards adopting a company policy and culture that is, within operational requirements, committed to harm minimisation. The greater the adoption of this attitude throughout the industry, the greater the probability that it will have a significant role in the curtailment of problem gambling in the UK.

Education and Awareness

It seems to me there are three main methods of problem prevention that can be applied. The first is that of prohibition which, in an open society, as the Americans discovered in trying to ban alcohol, is an impossibility and creates new problems by encouraging criminality. The same is true of gambling, as can be illustrated by the legalisation of off-course bookmaking in 1960 when it was realised that prohibiting the activity was totally ineffective and was undermining respect for the law.

Second, an activity can be allowed in very controlled circumstances with the imposition of severe penalties for those that transgress the rules. Unfortunately, this again has proved to be relatively ineffective in an open society, as may be illustrated by the open flouting of stringent laws under the Obscene Publications Act. Enormous resources are necessary to check abuses of the law when a covert industry is flourishing because of huge popular demand. A point of compromise is reached which becomes deregulation by expediency. One of the stronger arguments for the introduction of a national lottery in Britain was to counter the embryonic growth of foreign lotteries in this country.

The third means of problem prevention is that of education and awareness. Whilst it will never eliminate all problems, trusting people to make their own decision from a position of informed choice is widely considered to be effective by helping agencies. For example, whilst it appears that the approach to drug use in the UK is that of prohibition, a different perspective is gained when you talk with agencies working on the ground. They will tell you that the most effective method of problem prevention is that of enabling people to make an informed choice in conjunction with sensible, enforceable regulation. I believe the same is true of gambling, and even more so because drugs are mainly illegal whilst gambling is very definitely an 'approved' societal activity.

Young people in particular need to be given information that enables them to decide for themselves whether they wish to gamble, which activities are most attractive, and which activities they need to be most careful about. Having established that it is not productive to say 'Don't do it', teenagers who are approaching an age where they are keen to try out this 'adult' activity of gambling need to be informed as to how best to stay in control. There are many methods of ensuring that the message is put across, and one obvious one is to use the formal education system. In 1997, in conjunction with an education adviser, I compiled a manual – *A Certain Bet* – that could be used as a dip-in pack with the Personal and Social Education (PSE) aspect of the secondary school curriculum (Bellringer and Haslar 1999). The following extract of an exercise for a teacher to undertake illustrates the type of educational material that will encourage young people to think for themselves about their gambling and also inform them as to how best to stay in control.

Graffiti Wall

Pin on the wall around the room large sheets of paper and on each write one of the following statements:

'When I gamble I ....'

'When I lose I ....'

'When I win I ....'

'When I have spent £1 in a fruit machine I ....'

'When I have spent 15 minutes playing on a slot machine I ....'

'Gambling makes me feel ....'

'Watching the National Lottery draw makes me feel ....'

Ask the pupils to walk round the room adding their own one or two word completion of the statement. For those that do not gamble ask them to imagine that they do. On completion take each sheet in turn and conduct a short discussion on their responses to the statements, highlighting common reactions.

Keeping control of your gambling is a message that all of us who do gamble need to keep in mind, especially at that time when it is most difficult ... the heat of the moment when you are carried away with the excitement and the atmosphere and *just know* that if you place a bet on this horse or that number you will win! The following guide that I have devised and which also appears in *A Certain Bet* is aimed particularly at young gamblers but, in fact, applies to everyone who has 'a punt'.

Whenever you gamble it is wise to remember that:

You are buying entertainment not investing your money. It is a mistake, except for those who are professional gamblers or those who see it as an extension of speculating on the financial markets, to see gambling as a means of making money. You are, in reality, buying fun, excitement, entertainment, and a win will add to these feelings. If you come out ahead at the end of a session that is a bonus, but on reflection it should be weighed against all the other occasions when you lost to get a true perspective as to whether you are making a profit.

You are unlikely to make money from gambling unless you spend time and energy studying form, are fortunate enough to be offered a tip that is 'a racing certainty', or are just plain lucky. The great majority of those of us who gamble lose more than we win – which is why it is a multi-million pound business and why those who do win consistently (such as the card counters in casinos) find themselves excluded from gambling establishments.

The gambling industry and the government are the real winners as despite the tax burden laid on the gambling industry there is a steady profit to be made. Latest figures suggest that from the estimated gambling turnover of £40 billion per annum, net revenue is some £3.5 billion and £900 million is profit (Topham and Donoughue 1998). As outlined in Chapter 1, the £1.7 billion slice taken in revenue plus a further £1.5 billion in money directed to good causes (providing indirect relief on treasury finances) makes gambling a real winner for the government.

You should only gamble with money you can afford to lose, which complements the point about buying entertainment. Using financial resources that are required to meet other obligations is a potential cause of trouble and immediately creates a mind-set that it is essential to win. When you have little spare cash, ask yourself how important is it to spend money on gambling as against something else that will meet a need.

You should set strict limits on how much you will gamble in order to ensure that gambling remains a social activity. Place a limit on how much you will spend on gambling before you start the session, and keep to it. Chasing losses and, to a smaller extent, the corollary of chasing winnings are strong factors in moving from social to problem gambling. As mentioned later on in this chapter, a choice also needs to be made as to whether money won will be added to the original amount or whether that will be reserved to be spent on something else.

To make a profit you should quit when ahead and as soon as this occurs. If you have set aside an amount to gamble this should not be supplemented by any winnings. These should be put in another pocket and spent on something else. The other aspect to remember if you want to make a profit is that like any other financial market the best chance of making money is to invest a great deal of time in studying all the factors that are likely to influence the outcome. In other words, the activity of gambling changes its nature; it moves away from the outright entertainment to a form of work.

Gambling should only take up a small amount of your time and interest as problem gamblers who become obsessed with gambling find that it occupies all their waking thoughts. To keep it under control, gambling should have its place in your life. It should be one of a range of interests and should occupy only a small part of your time. If this has been the case but gambling is now beginning to encroach increasingly on other matters, it is time to seriously reflect on how important this activity is becoming in your life.

Problems will arise if you become preoccupied with gambling and it assumes ever greater importance in your life. When it begins to take more of your time and attention, it will be at the expense of other people and other interests. Almost inevitably this will lead to problems in relationships, in carrying out responsibilities and obligations and, if the amount of expenditure on gambling also increases, in being able to live within your means.

Gambling within your means is likely to be fun and exciting as there is no doubt in my mind that many forms of gambling provide a great source of entertainment. Placing a stake against a horse, the turn of a card, the spin of the wheel, heightens the natural tension and anticipation associated with waiting for the imminent outcome of an event. To do this in the company of others who have also committed themselves to this risk creates an atmosphere that adds to the sense of occasion.

Gambling outside your means is likely to create serious problems both for you and for others. In addition to the problems outlined above, over-spending is perhaps the most potent factor that leads to that destructive downward spiral that epitomises the career of someone who is gambling dependent. Debt, dishonour, criminal conviction, imprisonment, degradation are powerful consequences that may result from gambling outside your means.

You should not gamble to escape from worries or pressures as the need to escape from problems and pressures is a powerful hook into developing a gambling dependency. Consequently, guarding against any motivation for gambling being that of escape (more than we all need to be entertained at times to forget everyday cares) is an important means of retaining control of the situation. Facing up to the pressure and then seeking entertainment through gambling as a way of rewarding yourself is in my view much healthier!

The feeling of being powerful and in control when gambling is largely a delusion, particularly in those activities that are entirely games of chance. The excitement and the action of competing against a machine or against the bookmaker can engender strong feelings of being in command of the situation. Whilst for that small number of highly skilled gamblers there is an element of truth in this reaction, the vast majority are deluding themselves if they get carried away with the thought that they are in control. Whilst it is good to chance your luck against the machine or roulette wheel, resist the idea that it is a competition where you are in charge – the reality is the opposite.

A gambling dependency is as damaging as other addictions and can have as devastating an effect on the life of the gambler or others as a dependency on alcohol or drugs, for example. Thinking that it is the 'lesser of the evils' is unlikely to bring any comfort for those who are affected by the dependency. Gambling, like alcohol, is a good servant but a very poor master.

Always gambling responsibly is a means of ensuring that it always remains in your control and stays an activity that brings good value for the money spent on it.

Quite apart from formal education, the other valuable means of raising awareness and helping to provide the opportunity for informed choice is the media. Television has for a number of years been the most powerful influence of all and, as technology improves, it is possible that the Internet will rival this medium as a source of influence.

Documentary-style programmes that highlight the pleasures alongside the pains associated with excessive gambling can do much to improve informed choice. Soaps, serials and dramas that feature gambling need to balance the glamour of the activity with a cautionary tale or message that reminds viewers of the risks involved. When that occurs routinely the message that gambling needs to be treated with respect will gain greater credence than I believe it currently commands.

Problem Gamblers and Prevention

Catching someone at the early stage of problem gambling and assisting those who have broken the dependency to maintain their progress are also forms of prevention.

For the individual on that slippery slope between social and problem gambling the strategies outlined in Chapter 7 are applicable. Giving the 'at risk' gambler insight into their motivation for gambling and raising their awareness to the danger can be very effective in preventing an escalation of the problem. Operators staffing the GamCare National Helpline (see Chapter 8) have noticed that gamblers who see the number on display in gambling venues such as the betting office will ring to check whether or not they have a problem. Using the checklist outlined earlier (see Chapter 9) is likely to ascertain the extent to which gambling appears to be a problem. If the onset of a problem is identified and the gambler is motivated to address the issue, the self-help strategies are likely to be sufficient to prevent a dependency developing.

In the case of a problem gambler who has successfully broken the dependency, the need is for relapse prevention; that long-term strategy to avoid slipping back into uncontrolled gambling. A relapse prevention strategy should include the following.

A limit on future gambling. I have already argued that, in my view, it is wrong to apply a hard and fast rule about abstinence for life or a return to controlled gambling (see Chapter 9), as it depends on the circumstances of each individual. Quite clearly, however, total abstinence from future gambling is the most effective means of relapse prevention. For many, this draconian step is not necessary and, having broken the dependency, a return to limited gambling is possible. The safety factor is increased when the return is to a softer form of gambling, such as a former roulette gambler avoiding a return to the casino but buying a ticket for the National Lottery. Whilst there may be little comparison in terms of meeting the needs that drove the person into problem gambling in the first place, it does enable the individual to participate 'normally' in a societal activity and to continue to experience the hope that gambling brings. Should former problem gamblers feel that they can cope with a return to the activity that led them into difficulties, they will need to take extra care and set very strict limits on the amount they gamble, the time they devote to it, and also avoid gambling alone.

Internalising cognitive learning. During the process of tackling the dependency gamblers who have undergone a period of integrative counselling will have been encouraged to look at how they react to situations and events and to change the way in which they respond. This needs to be maintained so that the self-examination of reaction to any given situation becomes a continuous process. Any lapse back into uncontrolled gambling is likely, in my opinion, to be preceeded by a reversion to old, ingrained reactions, especially in those situations where the former gambler feels threatened or vulnerable in some way. Therefore, in terms of relapse prevention there is a need to maintain self-awareness and to reflect on how they react to given situations.

Watching for triggers. I hold the view that in certain circumstances we can all be vulnerable to narrowing our focus in the spectrum of dependencies. Somebody who has experienced a dependency is clearly at risk of returning to the same or a similar pattern of behaviour when they feel under particular pressure. Being able to identify during the course of recovery those triggers that increase the urge to gamble should not only assist the change process but also provide key information for the future. Avoidance of some triggers – for example, not watching the horse racing on television – is a powerful aid to relapse prevention. Equally important is to adapt and extend the awareness gained – for example, by choosing to face up to problems as they occur rather than running away from them.

Nurturing self-esteem. Similar to the process of change having a strong strand of raising the problem gambler's level of self-esteem, it is essential that this is maintained as a guard against relapse. I recall an instance of a young problem gambler who was attending a group to address his dependency. He seemed to be making good progress until he failed his driving test, which triggered a massive lapse into heavy gambling. Encouraged to retake the test quickly he passed at this second attempt. The status this gave him and the fact that this also opened up a job opportunity provided such a boost to his self-esteem that gambling soon became a thing of the past for him. Feeling good about themselves is often singled out by former problem gamblers as a factor in the maintenance of a gambling-free lifestyle. Adapting thought processes and interests in life so that the increased level of self-esteem can be sustained mutes the urge to seek solace through gambling. Indeed, the fact that the individual did have a problem that they have successfully overcome can work in this regard. The former problem gambler can feel that they have achieved something that they sought but which eluded them through gambling.

A portfolio of interests. Having effected change in themselves and begun to focus on other interests in their lives, former problem gamblers need to consolidate this achievement. Whilst a single constructive interest may well replace the gambling and meet similar needs it is perhaps more prudent to develop a range of other interests. This strategy is likely to meet a broader span of needs and head off disaster if for any reason any one new-found interest ceases to be available or ceases to be attractive. If the former gambler has been reliant on a single interest that subsequently becomes unavailable the pressure to revert to gambling can increase significantly.

People power. Problem gambling has a serious and profound negative effect on relationships. This is true whether difficulty with relationships is a causal link for the gambling or whether the gambling has eroded the ability to form satisfying bonds with other people. Exchanging the superficial interreaction with people for genuine bonds of deep emotional involvement, or for mutual respect and communication with friends and work colleagues, is an important strand in relapse prevention. For many former problem gamblers this will never be an easy process but the reward in making progress with human intercourse is clearly worth seeking. It also works in the sense of a former problem gambler being valued by fellow humans for their contribution as a leader, as a member of a team and as an individual and does much to underpin their recently retrieved sense of self-worth.

The money factor. In the eyes of society money is equated with power and status and the value placed on material success is magnified in the mind of the problem gambler. Reassessing the role of money in their lives can be an important part of the process of breaking the dependency and avoiding a relapse. It may be that there is a mountain of debt to pay off that will affect their spending power for years to come, but this burden can have a beneficial side. It meets the need to 'pay back' for what has been taken and can act as a spur to re-evaluating what money means in their life. Whilst money will always have significance, being able to mentally reduce its value as an indicator of personal status is likely to provide a further bulwark against returning to a lifestyle focussed on gambling.

Let's talk about it. Problem gamblers become very secretive individuals and hide their feelings and their thoughts from those to whom they are closest. Even when the dependency has been broken, continuing to talk through aspects of their chaotic gambling can provide further insight and help prevent a relapse. This should not, of course, be done obsessively but the occasional return to consider why they gambled should strengthen and consolidate change. It is important to share thoughts and feelings when there is a specific pressure evident, particularly when that pressure can be identified as one which in the past led to an intensification of gambling.

SUMMARY

If problem gambling is to be kept at a low level, regulation should reflect the need for harm minimisation, and this issue must be taken seriously by the gambling industry. Education programmes will provide the means whereby a gambler is able to make an informed choice and should contribute to problem prevention. Relapse prevention programmes should assist those who have experienced a dependency on gambling to reduce the likelihood of the problem returning.

CHECKLIST

The good gambling guide. Problems are likely to be avoided when a gambler keeps control of the situation and ensures that it remains a social activity. The following guide, aimed particularly at young gamblers but applicable to everyone, will help to ensure that gambling remains an enjoyable, problem-free experience. It is wise to remember that:

- You are buying entertainment, not investing your money.
- You are unlikely to make money from gambling.
- The gaming industry and the government are the real winners.
- You should only gamble with money you can afford to lose.
- You should set strict limits on how much you will gamble.
- To make a profit you should quit when ahead.
- Gambling should only take up a small amount of your time and interest.
- Problems will arise if you become preoccupied with gambling.

- Gambling within your means is likely to be fun and exciting.

- Gambling outside your means is likely to create serious problems.

- You should not gamble to escape from worries or pressures.

- The feeling of being powerful and in control when gambling is a delusion.

- A gambling dependency is as damaging as other addictions.

- Always gamble responsibly.

Relapse Prevention. Having successfully broken a dependency on gambling it is important to devise a strategy that will strengthen change and guard against a relapse. Useful elements of such a strategy are likely to include the following:

- Place a limit on future gambling, or avoid gambling altogether.

- Internalise learning and avoid reverting to ingrained reactions to difficult or stressful situations.

- Watch for situations and circumstances that trigger the urge to gamble and be ready to face them.

- Nurture self-esteem – work at feeling good about yourself.

- Develop a range of interests that, preferably, meet similar needs to those that were previously being met by gambling.

- Spend time and energy working at building good human relationships.

- Reassess the significance of money and endeavour to reduce its importance in your life.

- Continue to explore, on occasion, reasons why gambling became so significant in your life.

14 Addressing the Social Impact of Gambling

*As a caring society, we must not ignore the human misery
which gambling can cause, nor the social consequences
of excessive gambling.*

(Lord Williams, 1997)

As has been propounded throughout this book, gambling is a stylised form of natural human behaviour. Its formal acceptance within society legitimises an activity which would otherwise flourish underground. Because it is an activity that stirs up passion and excitement that is linked to material loss or gain, it creates a heady mix of feelings and responses. This can very definitely help to produce that much sought-after feel good factor which is measurably increased when a gambler wins.

Significant sums of money are involved that are attractive not only to the gambler but also to the businessman, the government and to the wider community. Many traditional gambling enterprises have arisen through generations of showman families or flamboyant individuals. Monarchs and governments have for centuries sanctioned and controlled gambling as a means of raising money for particular projects or, more recently, as a means of regular taxation. Gambling empires have been built up which, when strictly controlled, have enabled successful business enterprises to grow, but, when not so well regulated, gambling as a money-generating business tends to attract the criminal elements of society. Large corporate institutions are now becoming involved with the running of gambling business as it continues to expand on a global scale.

A strong attraction to gambling, the way it is 'packaged' and the enticement to take a chance can unfortunately combine to lead a number of gamblers to focus upon the activity with a greater intensity than is healthy. Problem gambling has a devastating effect on the individual, on a number of other people within the family, and on the wider community. The social cost of problem gambling is, in my experience, high in terms of the stress it places on individuals and families and the drain on society's resources.

The Growth of Gambling

In my opinion the social impact of gambling is greatly underestimated. By way of example let us take a look at the introduction of the National Lottery in the UK. As I outlined in Chapter 1, this has proved to be a catalyst for change and has been instrumental in turning gambling into a mainstream leisure activity.

In terms of social impact, this growth of gambling has had the following effects.

Increased turnover and per capita expenditure. With the total turnover of gambling now exceeding £40 billion per annum the average amount staked on gambling per adult (based on 46 million) is £870 a year.

Increased revenue for the treasury. Despite alterations to the tax rates the amount of money that goes to the treasury increases year on year. From the total take in tax and duty of £1.75 billion per annum (see Chapter 1) the Lottery contributes around a third of that amount.

An increase in the number of people gambling. Further research scheduled to take place in 1999 should provide a clearer idea as to who gambles on what and how frequently, but it has already been established (Mintel 1995) that the number of adults who gamble has risen to almost 91 per cent since the introduction of the National Lottery. What is more, many of those that had a once-a-year flutter on the Grand National or the Derby now regularly buy a draw ticket or a scratchcard.

More advertising. The rules regarding advertising, particularly of hard gambling activities, have until recently been draconian. The wide degree of promotional freedom granted to the National Lottery made mockery of that policy and is proving to be a yardstick for the rest of the industry.

Social gambling is now widely approved and popular. As discussed earlier in the book, the image and perception of gambling has changed within the span of a few years. The somewhat unwholesome label attached to gamblers has disappeared. Many people who participate in the Lottery either believe or rationalise their behaviour by saying that it is not really gambling.

An increase in problem gambling. Even supposing the percentage of problem gamblers has remained constant, given the rise in the number of people gambling there will have been a proportionate rise of those experiencing difficulty. However, it is my view that the availability and acceptability of gambling is having the unwanted effect of increasing that percentage.

An attraction for both adults and children. Without doubt, gambling has increased in popularity among adults, but a growing number of children are also finding it attractive. Fruit machines have traditionally been the most popular activity but both the National Lottery and scratchcards are causing interest in the younger age group.

A shake-out of market share. The National Lottery had an immediate impact on other gambling activities. The football pools industry has still not recovered from the body-blow dealt by the introduction of the National Lottery, and the off-course betting industry struggled for some while to regain market share.

The exposure of increasingly outdated legislation. The growth in gambling of the last few years and the increased pace of technological advancement has exposed the legislative framework. It is a question of when rather than if there will be a wholesale review of the laws and regulations concerning gambling.

The development of a gambling culture. There is no doubt in my mind that this growth of gambling driven by the introduction of the National Lottery and coupled with the process of relaxing current regulations has created a gambling culture on a far bigger scale than ever before seen in the UK.

Greatly increased availability. There was a time when, apart from the fruit machine in the corner of the fish and chip shop, you had to actively seek out the opportunity to gamble. The situation today has been turned on its head. If you wish to avoid being confronted with the opportunity to gamble it is, I would suggest, difficult if you live in a rural area, and nigh-on impossible in town.

These elements have been instrumental to the change in society's perception of gambling as well as intensifying the impact of this particular activity in the lives of the majority of people in the UK.

Early Attempts to Address Social Impact Issues

Given the inherent danger of some forms of gambling, the question we should all be asking is, has sufficient attention been given to the social impact of this growth? In a word, the answer is no. Let me sketch out a brief history of the response to the social impact of gambling.

If we take just this century, as far as I am aware prior to the 1960s there was no organisation that specifically addressed these issues. It must be said, however, that Police Court Missionaries, which later evolved into the probation service, and other groups working with the poor, the suffering and the distressed undoubtedly tried to mitigate the consequences of problem gambling. Some religious sects roundly denounced the evils of gambling but as far as I know did little to address the issues involved.

As mentioned in Chapter 10, GA was established during the early 1960s in the UK. This self-help organisation together with its sister Gam-Anon have, until very recently, been the mainstay of social impact provision. However, because of their code of anonymity GA does not offer an opinion on gambling and it relies on attraction to, rather than promotion of, its cause. Consequently, whilst its contribution is significant it is not in a position to address the broader issues or to significantly influence debate.

The Reverend Gordon Moody was a remarkable man who for several decades could be described as the guiding beacon in any response to the social impact of gambling. Following his success in setting up GA, he was involved in forming the National Council on Gambling to act as a watchdog on issues concerning legislation and regulation. Although this charity is technically still in existence, its current contribution to the debate on gambling issues is negligible. Gordon Moody next turned his attention to the plight of homeless problem gamblers, especially those whose addiction had led them into criminality. The Gordon House hostel (see Chapter 11) that was opened for these men in 1971 has certainly met the social consequence at this end of the social impact spectrum.

In an attempt to make some provision for families, Gordon Moody was also heavily involved in setting up Parents of Young Gamblers during the 1980s. This organisation continues, I understand, to provide a limited service, mostly in the Midlands area.

Also in the 1980s the Society for the Study of Gambling was founded as a 'Chatham House rules' forum (that is, not reportable or attributable) for debate and presentation of papers for everyone interested in the subject of gambling. There is no doubt that this society provides an important strand within the social framework by airing and sharing relevant views, theories and practices but, by its very nature, it cannot be anything other than a sounding board.

At the end of the 1980s a small number of local level youth counselling agencies, such as the Matthew Project in Norwich, began to include problem gambling in their repertoire. These developed as a response to a rise in the number of requests for help following the explosive growth of slot machines in the UK. However, these were ad hoc arrangements directly reacting to need and as such were fragmented and unco-ordinated.

The UK Forum on Young People and Gambling

It became increasingly obvious to me and to other people working in the field of gambling that there was a need for a national organisation that specifically addressed the social impact of gambling and which was able to respond to rising concern about the apparent growth of problems associated with young people playing fruit machines.

A series of meetings led to the creation, in 1990, of the UK Forum on Young People and Gambling, a registered charity with the following objectives:

- To promote public education and training about young people and gambling.

- To help rehabilitate and educate young persons who had or could develop a gambling problem.

- To promote or assist in the promotion of research into and information about the problems and issues arising from young people and gambling.

- To provide a network of contacts for those associated, or working, with young people who had or could have a gambling problem.

Its work covered the whole range of gambling activities available in the UK. The trend towards increased opportunities for young people to gamble and the promotion of gambling as an acceptable activity for all the family, highlighted concerns and intensified the need for education and problem prevention programmes.

As the charity developed its work it became clear that there was a definite link between gambling machines and electronic video machines and those issues were incorporated in the response of the UK Forum. However, it did not condemn gambling or the playing of electronic games as activities. Neither did it seek to restrict the choice of gambling activity available to young adults, nor the opportunities for all age groups to play electronic games.

However, it was concerned about the real damage done to some young people's lives and had a commitment to reduce the possibility of further damage. This was achieved by promoting responsible attitudes to gambling and working for the provision of proper care for those young people who had been harmed by these activities.

The charity became a forum for co-ordination, discussion and the development of strategies to reduce potential and actual harm to young people from gambling and, indeed, from electronic game-playing.

This first attempt to create a national co-ordinated body to address the social impact of gambling managed some success over its seven-year life, but was hampered by a number of factors, including those listed below.

Lack of adequate resources. At the time the UK Forum was set up there was little awareness as to the need for such a service. It was yet another charity chasing the same pot of money along with thousands of others. Consequently it struggled to survive and limited resources curtailed the work that could be done.

Lack of government will. The arrival of the charity coincided with a time when the government was minded to deregulate and, indeed, to expand the gambling industry. Whilst this should have created a positive response to social impact issues it became clear that the government was shy about considering the negative effects of gambling.

Industry suspicion. Despite demonstrating a gambling-neutral stance the gambling industry as a whole was deeply suspicious about the motives of the UK Forum. The few enlightened members of betting and gaming companies or trade associations faced internal opposition from those that wished to deny their products might be the cause of problem gambling.

In retrospect the real value of the UK Forum was that of laying a solid foundation for what was to come, in establishing the notion that such an organisation is needed in a society that allows widespread gambling, and in making some progress in allaying the suspicions of at least some sectors of the gambling industry.

The catalyst of change that occurred following the introduction of the National Lottery brought the issues into sharp focus. It provided the opportunity for the social impact of gambling to be reassessed and for a broader-based and better-resourced charity to be established.

National Association for Gambling Care, Educational Resources and Training (GamCare)

It was, in my view, important that any such organisation would command widespread respect and would maintain a neutral stance on gambling. The spur to action came from Nigel Kent-Lemon, the then Managing Director of London Clubs, who challenged those involved with the social impact of gambling to work more closely with the gambling industry.

I responded by bringing together a small number of people whose interests and experience represented a range of interests within the field of gambling. Nigel Kent-Lemon was one of this number and, until his untimely death in December 1998, was totally committed to the development of an effective and successful national organisation. It was quickly established among us that there was a need for an adequately resourced national service on gambling, acting as a unified body to be:

- A source of reliable information about gambling issues in order to enable people to make an informed choice with regard to gambling and to help break down myth and misinformation.

- A resource for advice in regard to government, the gambling industry, those community groups working with the issues, and those affected by a gambling dependency.

- A centre of a national group of services providing facilities for problem gamblers both in regard to developing GamCare's own response and in assisting and encouraging others.

- A lead body in devising and developing relevant practice standards for counsellors and practitioners working with those affected by a gambling dependency in order to achieve effectiveness, consistency, correlation with approaches to other dependencies, and a means of improving service provision.

- A co-ordinator for a national network of individuals and organisations interested in the social impact of gambling so that a growing number of agencies and people could be kept informed of relevant issues, to create a ready point of reference, and to be an aid in achieving good practice.

- A conduit for resources so that requests from those who sought help or support in developing a social impact response could be assessed and assisted as appropriate.

- A contributor to an environment for shared learning and understanding with regard to the social impact of gambling in order to further debate the issues, to create a climate for discussion and to encourage inclusion of consideration of these issues into policy and practice decisions by all sections of society.

- A voice of authority with regard to social impact issues to help decision makers in society to formulate a balanced strategy in regard to the development of gambling in the UK.

By the end of 1996 a constitution had been drawn up, charitable status and registration as a company limited by guarantee had been obtained and financial support was being sought. With considerable help across a broad spectrum of the gambling industry and a National Lottery Charities Board grant (originally awarded to the UK Forum on Young People and Gambling until its merger with the new charity), GamCare became operational at the beginning of April 1997. It began to realise the functions outlined above and very quickly achieved its first objective of becoming the national centre for information, advice and practical help with regard to the social impact of gambling.

Aims

The charity has evolved three specific aims. Each of these relate to the development of understanding how gambling can become a problem and how that harm can be minimised. These cover an area that has previously been neglected or unco-ordinated:

- **To improve the understanding of the social impact of gambling.** As I have pointed out during the course of this book, whilst there have been some attempts to focus on this aspect of gambling nothing has previously been attempted in a concerted manner. With the recent repositioning of gambling in society, the increasing attractiveness and popularity of this activity and the global growth of gambling it has become more important than ever that the impact is understood and responded to appropriately.

- **To promote a responsible approach to gambling.** It is essential, in my view, that a balanced view of gambling is further developed and maintained. Allowing it to flourish unchecked or going to the other extreme by driving it underground through suppression will create a climate of exploitation and a high incidence of problem gambling. Responding to this natural proclivity in a way that balances freedom of choice with responsibility provides a way forward for all sections in society that have an interest in gambling. This should also have the beneficial effect of minimising harm.

- **To address the needs of those adversely affected by a gambling dependency.** Whether we like it or not, gambling carries inherent dangers and for a significant minority it becomes a very destructive addiction. Facilities for helping those so afflicted remain relatively sparse and under-developed. The need is to develop a range of facilities so that they are known, available and accessible through-out the UK.

The Work of GamCare

In order to carry through these aims the charity concentrates on four specific areas of work. These are:

Care

Of high priority must be dealing with the consequences of problem gambling. Spearheading the care aspect of the work of GamCare is its national helpline (see Chapters 8 and 15). This service, staffed by trained volunteers and supervised by qualified counsellors, provides the first point of contact for anyone affected by a gambling dependency. It is used frequently by family members as well as by problem gamblers. Those in crisis and in desperate need of help have access to a dedicated helpline from which they can derive comfort, reassurance, advice, information, support and encouragement to address the dependency.

Backing up the national helpline is GamCare's own free, confidential counselling service which is undertaken by trained counsellors who are supervised by a counselling manager. This integrative approach is based on motivational interviewing and a cognitive behavioural method of enabling the problem gambler and/or family member effectively to break free of the dependency. Following an assessment interview four to six sessions are usually offered. The stage the counselling has reached will then be assessed and a further number of sessions may be offered if it is agreed that it would be beneficial to look further at issues related to the gambling dependency. As a specialised service it has, of necessity, to maintain the focus on gambling but the counselling process may well reveal other issues that the gambler wishes to explore.

In these instances the charity endeavours to link the gambler with another agency that can take the process forward.

Because the charity is London-based, realistically only those who can comfortably travel into the capital can avail themselves of this service. Consequently GamCare is developing a network of appropriate counselling agencies throughout the UK. These agencies may be offering a broad range of help such as that provided by a youth counselling centre, or may offer a more specialised service such as that provided by a drug and alcohol agency. In a growing number of selected areas where provision for addressing a gambling dependency is poor, GamCare is setting up specific joint venture projects with suitable agencies already working in the field of addictive behaviours.

As this network strengthens, callers to the helpline will increasingly be able to be referred to a local counselling service that can confidently address a gambling dependency. For many callers this will provide an element of choice between a local counselling service and Gamblers Anonymous and, as I pointed out in Chapter 10, the opportunity to gain insight from the one and support from the other.

Education

The second strand of the work of GamCare concerns education. Whilst this may be aimed primarily at young people it is by no means exclusive to that generation. Adults also need to be able to make an informed choice and to follow the same guidelines for keeping gambling as a social activity as do the younger generations. For example, the portrayal of the National Lottery as 'not really gambling' has been, in my mind, a considerable factor in the high incidence of selling lottery products to children under the age of 16. Parents do not see it as a form of gambling and so encourage their children or buy the products on their behalf. Neither do they see it as being harmful on their own account, even though there are instances where buying the weekly draw ticket or, more often, the scratchcard has become an obsession.

Consequently, one focus of the educational message is to raise the awareness of relevant issues. The widespread dissemination of accurate balanced information can make a significant contribution to informed choice. For those still within the formal education process the charity has produced a manual that can be used as part of the personal and social education aspect of the national curriculum. Similarly, youth organisations have access to an activity-based trigger pack. Callers to the helpline or those making a general enquiry are able to request a range of material that provides information on the issues. Articles ranging from the perspective of the gambling industry to a personal account by a problem gambler are covered in the charity's magazine which has increasing circulation among GamCare's network of members, regulators, government departments, the gambling industry and others.

As gambling is a constant source of interest to the media this provides an effective channel of communication by which to get across the issues. Television, radio, newspapers and magazines all help to raise awareness of gambling issues and to reach those people who need to reflect on how gambling is affecting them. Within the context of media outlets, specifically targeted advertising will reinforce the message.

All of these means of communication provide opportunities to promote responsible gambling. At the heart of the balance between freedom of choice and personal responsibility lies the commitment to keep gambling under control as an occasional social activity. The gambling guide (see Chapter 13) is included in a range of educational material that includes leaflets as well as manuals and trigger packs designed for use by young people. In addition to the charity directly promoting responsible gambling it also encourages the industry to do the same. Regardless of the fact that the gambling industry might be responding out of vested self-interest, their promotion of responsible gambling is likely to have a significant influence on their own customers. Similarly, an informative website nestling among all the Internet gambling enticements can act as an important reminder of the need to retain control of the situation.

A central objective in raising awareness of the issues and in promoting responsible gambling is that of preventing problem gambling. Educating people about gambling is rather like that of education about drinking alcohol. It allows the active participant an opportunity to reflect on what they are doing. That, I am convinced, keeps many a gambler from allowing their social pastime to develop into something altogether more serious. For others it will have no impact during the denial stage of their gambling career but may play a part in relapse prevention once they have begun to address the dependency.

Training

Linked to both the previous strands is that of training. A range of courses have been written and are delivered by GamCare in order to raise awareness and to enhance the skills of those who are being trained. I am often surprised by the blank spot among the helping professions with regard to gambling and its consequences. Pitching training in a fashion that allows them to make links with other addictions and behaviours enables them to readily embrace the concepts and use the content as a tool for further work.

Very specific courses for helpline volunteers and for counsellors have been designed to enable them to work confidently with problem gamblers. Additionally, youth workers, probation officers, social workers, those in the health service, community workers and many others are able to benefit from relevant training. In keeping with GamCare's gambling neutrality it wishes to develop links right across the gaming industry. One means of doing this is to run awareness training courses for selected gambling industry staff and to encourage that awareness to cascade down to those having direct contact with the gambling customer.

Research

In order to influence the poor state of affairs with regard to good-quality research data the charity has also become involved in supporting and undertaking research that will lead to further understanding of the social impact of gambling. It is a strange state of affairs that allows the expansion of an activity that is known to bring pleasure on the one hand and to cause problems on the other without having the means to gauge the possible impact in terms of social cost.

The benefits to society in general, and to a local area in particular, should be researched, as should the extent to which any particular gambling activity is in itself a cause of problem gambling. For example, from my previous experience working in the criminal justice area I am aware that gambling is not often determined as the direct cause of criminality. However, I am convinced that it has a greater and more significant effect as a contributing factor in offending behaviour. The extent of this contribution needs to be researched.

This is but one area from a whole spectrum of research possibilities. However, the arrival of a national umbrella organisation working in conjunction with appropriate academic institutions and survey specialists creates a real possibility for reliable data to be determined, and for making a contribution to the formulation of future policy.

In a short space of time GamCare has occupied an important position in the general scheme of gambling within the UK. This has, in my mind, been assisted by the current government that has been prepared to listen and seek advice in keeping with its problem-solving and pragmatic approach to moving the country forward. GamCare provides a point of reference for all sections of society with an interest in gambling and provides a bridge between freedom of choice and responsibility. Whilst addressing the devastating consequences of problem gambling is a vitally important strand of its work, helping to prevent that slide from social to problem gambling is a key role for the charity.

One of the challenges of the twenty-first century for the UK will be to reassess the extent to which gambling should be allowed to develop and to decide what is the right balance between maximising opportunity and minimising harm. That challenge has been made easier by the existence of this national charity with a total focus on the social impact of gambling.

SUMMARY

The need for a co-ordinated response to the social impact of gambling has become increasingly necessary to match the steady growth of gambling that has occurred during the 1990s. The introduction of the National Lottery proved to be a catalyst in repositioning gambling as a mainstream leisure activity. Early attempts to address the issues centred on the continued efforts and energy of the Reverend Gordon Moody. He was involved in all significant endeavours that took place between the 1960s and 1990s. Since 1997, GamCare has become the national centre for information, advice and practical help with regard to the social impact of gambling in the UK.

CHECKLIST

Gambling in the UK has greatly increased during recent years because of a process of deregulation of the gambling industry and because of the introduction of the National Lottery. The social impact of this growth of gambling has been:

- Increased turnover and per capita expenditure.

- Increased revenue for the treasury.

- An increase in the number of people gambling.

- More advertising.

- Social gambling is now widely approved and popular.

- An increase in problem gambling.

- An attraction for both adults and children.

- A shake-out of market share.

- The exposure of increasingly outdated legislation.

- The development of a gambling culture.

- Greatly increased availability.

The National Association for Gambling Care, Educational Resources and Training, more commonly known as GamCare, has become the national centre for information, advice and practical help with regard to the social impact of gambling. It was founded in 1997 to be:

- A source of reliable information about gambling issues.

- A resource for advice.

- A centre of a national group of services providing facilities for problem gamblers.

- A lead body in devising and developing relevant practice standards for counsellors and practitioners working with those affected by a gambling dependency.

- A co-ordinator for a national network of individuals and organisations interested in the social impact of gambling.

- A conduit for resources.

- A contributor to an environment for shared learning and understanding with regard to the social impact of gambling.

- A voice of authority with regard to social impact issues.

15 Sources of Help and Further Information

*I thought I was alone with this problem. It's wonderful
to find someone who understands and can help.*

(Sarah – the wife of a problem gambler, aged 43)

Sources of help for this 'hidden addiction' are only just beginning to develop in a co-ordinated fashion. The long-established Gamblers Anonymous organisation and the Gordon House hostel for gamblers have for many years been virtually alone in coping with a problem that is undoubtedly as old as the phenomenon of gambling itself.

A number of such agencies have already been mentioned in this book but this chapter endeavours to draw together those in the UK that are currently active and which, as far as I am aware, have been accorded accountable and credible status. Other useful sources of information are included that concern the operation of gambling, its regulation, research or study.

DEDICATED HELPLINES FOR PROBLEM GAMBLERS

GamCare Helpline 0845 6000 133

This national 'lo-call' helpline, staffed by trained volunteers, is open twelve hours a day and provides support, information and counselling for anyone affected by a gambling dependency, and advice and assistance for practitioners who are working with a problem gambler.

Gamblers Anonymous 0171 384 3040

This national helpline, run by members of the Gamblers Anonymous fellowship and Gam-Anon, provides a 24-hour service for problem gamblers and their families. Callers are supported and encouraged to attend a Gamblers Anonymous or Gam-Anon meeting.

NATIONAL ORGANISATIONS WORKING EXCLUSIVELY WITH THE SOCIAL IMPACT OF GAMBLING

GamCare

25–27 Catherine Place, Westminster, London SW1E 6DU
Tel: 0171 233 8988
Fax: 0171 233 8977
e-mail: director@gamcare.org.uk
website: www.gamcare.org.uk

The national centre for information, advice and practical help in relation to the social impact of gambling. A pro-responsible gambling registered charity providing a national helpline; telephone and face-to-face counselling; a network of local counselling and support organisations; information and advice on social impact issues; training courses; leaflets, booklets, manuals and other literature; research; and consultancy services.

Gamblers Anonymous

PO Box 88, London SW10 0EU
Tel: 0171 384 3040

GA is a self-help fellowship of men and women who have joined together to do something about their own gambling problem and to help other compulsive gamblers to do the same. Over 200 groups throughout the UK and Eire and in many prisons. Meetings on one or more nights a week in many cities and towns. Literature available on request.

Gam-Anon

PO Box 88, London SW10 0EU
Tel: 0171 384 3040

'Sister' organisation to GA providing support and advice to the partners and parents of compulsive gamblers. Large number of groups throughout UK and Eire meet on same night but separate from Gamblers Anonymous meeting. Literature available on request.

RESIDENTIAL FACILITIES FOR PROBLEM GAMBLERS

Gordon House Association

186 Mackenzie Road, Beckenham Kent BR3 4SF
Tel: 0181 778 3331
Also located at Dudley, West Midlands

With a national catchment area this registered charity provides a dedicated residential facility for males aged 18 and over. Admittance following assessment period for a nine-month programme and help to move back into the wider community. Offers a therapeutic environment, individual and group counselling and support both whilst at the House and after the resident has left.

Lincolnshire Probation Service Residential Centre

205 Yarborough Road, Lincoln, LN1 3NQ
Tel: 01522 528520

Within its range of residential services has allocated bed spaces for identified problem gamblers who are subject to a criminal court order. Addresses the problems presented by offenders who are compulsive gamblers or whose offending behaviour is linked to problematic gambling.

Private Clinics

Promis Recovery Centre

The Old Court House, Pinners Hill, Nonington, Kent, CT15 4LL
Tel: 01304 841700

Addresses a number of dependencies including gambling. Uses the twelve-step programme.

Charter Nightingale Hospital

Lisson Grove, London NW1
Helpline: 0800 783 0594

Includes gambling addiction in its portfolio of treatment services. Uses the twelve-step programme.

Priory Hospital

Priory Lane, Roehampton, London SW15 5JJ
Tel: 0181 876 8261

Has 15 centres in its group. Treatment for a range of addictions including problem gambling. Uses the twelve-step model.

LOCAL/REGIONAL ORGANISATIONS OFFERING SPECIALISED COUNSELLING TO PROBLEM GAMBLERS

There are a growing number of adult- and youth-focused agencies that have counsellors who are able to work confidently with someone who has a gambling dependency. Those listed below can offer contact with counsellors and/or psychologists who specialise in working with this addiction.

GamCare

25–27 Catherine Place, Westminster, London SW1E 6DU
Tel: 0171 233 8988

Assessment and up to twelve face-to-face sessions based on an integrative approach to counselling. A free, confidential service for problem gamblers and family members. Available to anyone who can travel to its central London counselling centre.

Community Health Sheffield NHS Trust

Specialist Psychotherapy Directorate, Brunswick House,
299 Glossop Road, Sheffield S10 2HL
Tel: 0114 271 6890

For problem gamblers in the Sheffield NHS Trust area and may take referrals from outside this area. Short-term treatment of around 15 sessions based on an integrative counselling approach. Referral from a doctor is required.

Pathfinder Mental Health Services NHS Trust

Department of Psychology, Springfield Hospital, Glenburnie Road, Tooting, London SW17
Tel: 0181 672 9911

Referral from a doctor or source of agreed funding required. Offers assessment and an open-ended number of sessions that are periodically reviewed. Cognitive behavioural approach. Self-help support group also available.

Cumbria Alcohol and Drug Advisory Service (CADAS)

1 Fisher Street, Carlisle, Cumbria, CA3 8RR
Tel: 01228 544140

Provides a local telephone helpline and one-to-one counselling service for problem gamblers and their relatives and friends, as well as dealing with other addictive behaviours. Offers an integrative counselling approach. Will take referrals outside Cumbria from people affected by a gambling dependency.

North East Council on Addiction (NECA)

Phillipson House, 5 Phillipson Street, Walker,
Newcastle-upon-Tyne NE6 4EN
Tel: 0191 234 3486

Provides a telephone and one-to-one counselling service for problem gamblers and their relatives and friends as part of the service they offer at eleven centres around the county of Durham. Will take referrals outside this area from people affected by a gambling dependency.

Alcohol Problem Advisory Service (APAS)

36 Park Row, Nottingham, NG1 8GP
Tel: 0115 941 4747

Provides an advice, information and counselling service for those who have a, or are affected by someone else's, dependency on alcohol, drugs or gambling.

The Matthew Project

24 Pottergate, Norwich, Norfolk, NR2 1DX
Tel: 01603 626123

Provides an advice and counselling service to young gamblers who make contact or who are referred.

SPECIALIST DEBT COUNSELLING AGENCIES

National Debtline: 0645 500 511

The Birmingham Settlement
318 Summer lane, Birmingham B19 3RL

A long-established source of advice and help for those in debt or experiencing financial difficulties.

Citizens' Advice Bureau – See your local telephone directory

Provides advice and help with regard to debt and financial difficulties.

UMBRELLA ORGANISATIONS THAT HAVE AN INTEREST IN OR CARRY INFORMATION ABOUT THE SOCIAL IMPACT OF GAMBLING

Youth Access

1A Taylor's Yard, 67 Alderbrook Road, London SW12 8AD
Tel: 0181 772 9900

Co-ordinating agency for a national youth counselling network. Can advise on which youth counselling projects have counsellors available that have been trained in regard to a gambling dependency.

Youth Clubs UK

2nd Floor, Kirby House, 20–24 Kirby Street, London EC1N 8TS
Tel: 0171 242 4045

Co-ordinating agency for voluntary sector youth associations. Has information on those clubs and associations that have developed work around gambling issues.

National Council for Social Concern

Montague Chambers, Montague Close, London SE1 9DA
Tel: 0171 403 0977

Produces educational materials for church schools and youth organisations. Covers gambling issues in its range of information and advice.

Methodist Church

Division of Social Responsibility
1 Central Buildings, Westminster, SW1H 9NH

Includes gambling within the range of topics of interest to the Methodist church.

GOVERNMENT DEPARTMENTS AND ORGANISATIONS CONCERNED WITH THE REGULATION OF GAMBLING

The Home Office

Constitutional and Community Policy Department
Liquor, Gambling and Data Protection Unit
50 Queen Anne's Gate, London SW1H 9AT
Tel: 0171 273 2707

Department with responsibility for all forms of gambling except the National Lottery and those regulated under the Financial Services Act.

Gaming Board for Great Britain

Berkshire House, 168–173 High Holborn, London WC1V 7AA
Tel: 0171 306 6200

Principal regulating authority for gambling with responsibility for casinos, slot machines, bingo and society lotteries.

Department of Culture Media and Sport (DCMS)

2–4 Cockspur Street, London SW1Y 5DN
Tel: 0171 211 6000

Government department responsible for the National Lottery.

National Lottery Commission (NLC)

2 Monck Street, London SW1P 2BQ
Tel: 0171 227 2000

Regulating authority for the conduct of the National Lottery.

THE GAMBLING INDUSTRY:
MAJOR ASSOCIATIONS AND GROUPS

British Amusement Catering Trades Association (BACTA)

BACTA House
Regents Wharf, 6 All Saints Street, London N1 9RQ
Tel: 0171 713 7144

Association for all aspects of the slot machine industry.

British Casino Association

29 Castle Street, Reading, Berkshire, RG1 7SL
Tel: 0118 958 9191

Association for all British casinos.

Betting Office Licensees Association

3a Lower James Street, London W1R 3PN
Tel: 0171 434 2111

Association for the majority of off-course bookmakers.

The Bingo Association

5th Floor, Goldsmith's House,
137 Regent Street, London W1R 7LD
Tel: 0171 287 3611

Association for bingo club operators.

The Pools Promoters Association

100 Old Hall Street, Liverpool, L3 9TD
Tel: 0151 227 4181

Association for football pools operators.

UNIVERSITIES WITH DEPARTMENTS OR INDIVIDUALS STRONGLY INVOLVED WITH GAMBLING ISSUES

Centre for Gambling and Commercial Gaming

**Salford University
Adelphi House, The Crescent, Salford M3 6EN
Tel: 0161 839 2820**

Runs a graduate course on the economics of gambling and produces information of value to the gambling industry.

Centre for Research into the Social Impact of Gambling

**University of Plymouth, Faculty of Human Sciences
Drake Circus, Plymouth, Devon PL4 8AA
Tel: 01752 233200**

A leading research institute in the social impact of gambling.

Psychology Division, Depart of Social Science

**Nottingham Trent University,
Burton Street, Nottingham NG1 4BU
Tel: 0115 941 8418**

Undertakes extensive research in the field of gambling.

OTHER

The Society for the Study of Gambling

**Secretary: Paul Bellringer
(address as for GamCare)
Tel: 0171 233 8988**

References

Abt, V. and Smith, J.F. (1984) 'Gambling as Play', *Annals of the American Academy of Political and Social Science,* 474.

Bell, C. (1998) Extract from address given at Labour Party Conference 1998. *GamCare News* 4:15.

Bellringer, P. (1993) *Working with Young Problem Gamblers: Guidelines to Practice,* UK Forum on Young People and Gambling, London.

Bellringer, P. and Farman, J. (1997) *Young Gambling: A Guide for Parents,* National Association for Gambling Care, Educational Resources and Training, London.

Bellringer, P. and Fisher, S. (1997) *The Young Fruit Machine Player,* UK Forum on Young People and Gambling, London.

Bellringer, P. and Haslar, J. (1999) *A Certain Bet,* National Association for Gambling Care, Educational Resources and Training, London.

Browne, B.R. (1989) 'Going on the Tilt: Frequent Poker Players and Control', *Journal of Gambling Behaviour,* 3:21.

Callois, R. (1962) *Man, Play and Games,* Free Press, New York.

Chin, C. (1990) 'Betting Shops and Race by Race Betting Before the Betting and Gaming Act, 1960', *Society for the Study of Gambling Newsletter,* 17.

Devereux, E.C. (1949) 'Gambling and the Social Structure'. Doctoral dissertation. Harvard University.

Farrell-Roberts, K. (1997) 'Evaluating Effectiveness: Residents Satisfaction Survey'. Paper prepared for the Gordon House Association, London.

Fisher, S. (1991) *The Pull of the Fruit Machine: A Sociological Typology of Young Players.* University of Plymouth, England.

—— (1993) 'Gambling and Pathological Gambling In Adolescents', *Journal of Gambling Studies,* 9:277–88.

—— (1998) *Gambling and Problem Gambling among Young People in England and Wales.* Office of the National Lottery (OFLOT), London.

Fitzgerald, S. (1994) 'Gambling and the Law', *Society for the Study of Gambling Newsletter,* July, 25–9.

Gamblers Anonymous (1994) 'The Twelve Steps of Recovery', *Blue Book* (third edition). Gambler's Anonymous, USA.

—— (1996) *Questions to Ask.* Gamblers Anonymous, UK.

—— (1997) *Questions and Answers about the Problem of Compulsive Gambling and the GA Recovery Programme.* Gamblers Anonymous, UK.

Gaming Board for Great Britain (1994/95) 'Objectives of Regulation', *Annual Report.* HMSO, London.

Gaming Board for Great Britain (1997/98) 'The Organisation and Work of the Board: Why Gaming is Regulated and the Objectives of Regulation', *Annual Report*. HMSO, London.

Graham, J. (1988) *Amusement Machines: Dependency and Delinquency*. Home Office Report 101. HMSO, London.

Griffiths, M. (1991) 'Adolescent Fruit Machine Use: a Review of Current Issues and Trends', *UK Forum on Young People and Gambling Newsletter* 4:2–3.

—— (1995) *Adolescent Gambling*. Routledge, London.

http//www.worldwidelotteries.com Starnet Communications International inc.

Larkin, P. (1974) 'This Be The Verse', *High Windows*. Faber & Faber, London.

Lesieur, H.R. and Custer R.L. (1984) 'Pathological Gambling: Roots, Phases and Treatment', *Annals of the American Academy of Political and Social Sciences*, 474:146–56.

Lesieur, H.R. and Klein, R. (1987) 'Pathological Gambling Amongst High School Students', *Addictive Behaviours* (USA), 12:129–35.

Lesieur, H.R. and Rosenthal, R.J. (1991) 'Pathological Gambling: A Review of the Literature', *Journal of Gambling Studies*, 1:5–39.

Lorenz, V.C. (1994) 'Losses and Traumas as Precursors to Compulsive Gambling'. Paper presented to the Ninth International Conference on Gambling and Risk-Taking, Nevada, USA.

Lorenz, V.C. and Shuttleworth, D.E. (1983) 'The Impact of Pathological Gambling on the Spouse of the Gambler', *Journal of Community Psychology* (USA), 11:67–76.

Mintel (1995) *Survey on Post Lottery Gambling Behaviour*.

Moody, G. (1990) *Quit Compulsive Gambling*. Thorsens, London.

——London: (1994) 'The Roots, Significance and Value of Gambling', *Society for the Study of Gambling Newsletter* (special edition).

New Life (1995) (Journal of Gamblers Anonymous), October, p. 15.

New Life (1998) Preamble, July, p. 3.

'Peter' (1998) 'What is the Twelve Step Programme?' *GamCare News* 3:6.

Rosenfield, M. (1997) *Counselling by Telephone*. Sage, London.

Spanier, D. (1987) *Easy Money: Inside the Gambler's Mind*. ABACUS, London.

Steinberg, L. (1993) 'Running a Gambling Business – with a Moral Outlook', *UK Forum on Young People and Gambling Newsletter*, 8:2.

Steinberg, M.A. (1993) 'Couples Treatment Issues for Recovering Male Compulsive Gamblers and their Partners', *Journal of Gambling Studies*, 9:2.

'Sue' (1994) 'Is There a Gambling Problem in Your Home?', *UK Forum on Young People and Gambling Newsletter* 11:8–9.

TACADE (1992) *Basic Facts: Gambling*. TACADE, Manchester.

Topham, N. and Donoughue, S. (1998) 'The UK Gaming Industry 1996'. Report presented to the Industry Forum by Centre for the Study of Gambling and Commercial Gaming, Salford University, Manchester.

Twain, M. (1987) 'The £1,000,000 Bank Note', short story published in *The Laughter Omnibus*. Headline, London.

Williams, Lord (1997) Address delivered at the launch of the National Association for Gambling Care, Educational Resources and Training. London.

Wood, R. and Griffiths, M.D. (1998) 'The Acquisition, Development and Maintenance of Lottery and Scratchcard Gambling in Adolescence', *Journal of Adolescence*, 21:265–73.

World Health Organization (1995) *Classification of Mental and Behavioural Disorders*, WHO, Geneva.

Index

self-esteem
  building 118–19, 139, 141,
    172–3
  low 30–1, 38, 40–3, 58–9, 90
self-examination 129
self-help groups 107, 122,
    125–36
self-help strategies 89–90, 101–2
self-reward 90
Shuttleworth, D.E. 39
skill 2, 12, 21, 52
sleeplessness 34
slot machines 4, 7, 53
  chasing losses 28, 35, 55, 161
  growth of 8, 18
  and illusion of control 21, 54
  and money 17
  regulation 160
  see also fruit machines; young
    people
Smith, J.F. 15
Society for the Study of
    Gambling 179
Spanner, D. 16
sporting events 10
spread betting 11, 16
stealing 63, 68–9, 84, 143
  'borrowing' 28, 35, 116
  from family 63, 66, 73, 83
  thrill of 55
  see also criminal activity
Steinberg, L. 23
stock market 18
stress 42
suicide 36, 65, 70

taxation 2, 5
  source of government revenue
    8, 108, 176, 177
telephone betting 10
thrill 2, 17, 18–20, 31, 52–3,
    55–6, 115
Topham, N. 8

'tossing rings' 5
transactional analysis 118
twelve step recovery programme
    127–32
'two-up' 5

UK Forum on Young People and
    Gambling 95, 180–1

Varah, Rev Chad 93
vulnerability 30–2, 38, 59, 109
  see also dependency; family;
    gamblers, family background

winning
  effect of 32, 115
  phase 64
Wood, R. 50
World Health Organisation
    (WHO) 26

young people
  attraction of gambling 49, 51–3,
    59–61, 178
  'buzz' 52–3, 55–6
  and competitive sport 55–6
  and education 166–7
  and empowerment 52, 54–5
  encouraged to gamble 49, 57
  and escapism 52, 53–4
  and fruit machines 7, 50, 51,
    52, 53–6, 95
  and National Lottery 49–50,
    178
  and parental involvement
    148–52
  playing to win money 51–2
  and problem gambling 53–59,
    119, 180–1
  sociological factors 51
  underage gambling 164

Compiled by Sue Carlton